BENTLEY
4¹/₂-LITRE SUPERCHARGED

Autofolio

BENTLEY
4½ LITRE SUPERCHARGED

MICHAEL HAY

Autofolio

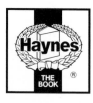

A **FOULIS** Motoring Book

First Published 1990

© Haynes Publishing Group 1990

Published by:
Haynes Publishing Group
Sparkford, Nr Yeovil, Somerset
BA22 7JJ

Haynes Publications Inc.
861 Lawrence Drive, Newbury Park,
California 91320, USA

British Library Cataloguing in Publication Data
Hay Michael
    Bentley 4.5-litre supercharged autofolio.
    1. Bentley supercharged 4.5 litre cars
    I. Title
    629.2222
    ISBN 0-85429-830-4

Library of Congress catalog card number
90-83285

Series Photographer: David Sparrow
Editor: Mansur Darlington
Book design: Camway Autographics
Printed in England by: J.H. Haynes & Co. Ltd
Typeset in 9/10pt Frontiera light roman

CONTENTS

The Supercharged 4½-Litre Bentley was unquestionably a supercar of the time, one that encapsulated the mechanical philosophies of an era that could be traced back to well before the First World War. Then, the vast, low-revving engines of the early racing cars had been displaced by the comparatively high revving, small capacity engines that were generally credited to Ernest Henri and Zuccarelli. Successful Grand Prix cars using Henri principles were developed and fielded principally by Peugeot and Mercedes, reaching their zenith at the French Grand Prix of 1914 when Mercedes finished first, second, and third. The 3-Litre Bentley was a direct road-going derivative of those Peugeots and Mercedes, and the Supercharged 4½-Litre a direct derivative of the 3-Litre. The Supercharged 4½-Litre marked the end of an era; an era of brute force and a degree of ignorance; it was a monumental road-going supercar that could still place second in the French Grand Prix 16 years after Mercedes' triumph.

Supercharging as a means of increasing the power of an engine enjoyed the same sort of vogue in the 1920s that turbocharging has enjoyed latterly. Either means of forced induction increases the engine power by pushing a larger volume of air/fuel mixture under pressure into the cylinders, thus releasing more power on ignition. Harnessing this added power sometimes requires extensive modification to the engine, but often engines of the 1920s were so understressed that a supercharger could be added with no alteration other than a drop in compression ratio. There is also the added glamour, a feature salesmen were as well ware of then as now. The nature of one's car may not have been writ in large letters along the bootlid, but nevertheless, visual changes were made to ensure that other people knew which model they were looking at. It may have been the use of wire wheels instead of disc, or the addition of stoneguards or extra bonnet louvres.

In the case of the Supercharged 4½-Litre Bentley the glamour came from the massive Roots-type supercharger projecting from below the radiator between the dumb-irons, flanked on the nearside by the twin SU carburettors and on the offside by the finned, cast aluminium trunking leading up to the inlet manifold. This somewhat brutal visual evidence of enhanced performance, backed up by the well-publicised activities of the Birkin/Paget team of Supercharged 4½-Litres, has ensured the model a place in history perhaps unmatched by any other British car of the era. That the glamorous image of the car was founded neither on commercial success when the car was new, nor on racing success of the model, makes the story of the supercharged or 'Blower' Bentleys even more interesting.

In the following pages, it is the author's intention to highlight the controversial background to the Blower cars, and the way in which that controversy threw a shadow over the model during its brief production life before Bentleys went to the wall in July 1931. The story inevitably covers the racing activities of the Birkin/Paget team, and perhaps shows why the Blower later acquired the image that it now possesses.

ACKNOWLEDGEMENTS

First and foremost, my thanks go to Tim Scott and Ted Parkinson for so generously putting up their cars for the comparison tests, and for allowing me to drive them. Secondly, to Stanley Mann, for putting up his Birkin 'Le Mans' replica, and to Coys and Harry Booth for, likewise, putting up their car. Thanks go to the Bentley Drivers' Club for access to their extensive archives, and to all those who have been quoted for the 'sidebars'. Finally my thanks to David Sparrow for the wonderful photographs.

The responsibility for the Supercharged 4½-Litre lies firmly with one man: Sir Henry Birkin, Bart, better known as Tim Birkin. Birkin was born into money, his family having made its fortune in Nottingham lace, and hence the young Birkin could afford to indulge his fancies. In the early 1920s he bought a DFP which he had tuned by Bentley & Bentleys, but for whatever reason it was not as fast as W.O.'s had been. (Bentley & Bentley was W.O. and H.M. Bentley's first company, set up in 1912, dealing in the French DFP car. It was with the 2-litre 12/15 DFP that W.O. started to make his name in competition.) With this car Birkin raced at Brooklands several times, but then retired from racing until 1927. He bought his first Bentley, a 3-Litre, in 1925, but did not race that car. He then bought another 3-Litre in 1927, built up to semi-Team Car

specification, and entered for the Essex Car Club's Six Hours Race at Brooklands in May of that year, partnered by his brother C.A.C. 'Archie' Birkin. The Birkin brothers' driving was rather wild, losing all the gears in the gearbox except third. The other team cars retired with broken rockers, due to a design fault in the new alloy components, only the Birkin car, fitted with the original steel rockers, still running. According to his autobiography *Full Throttle* (G.T. Foulis & Co., 1932) Tim was somewhat taken aback when Bertie Kensington-Moir, who was managing the pits, asked him to get out of the car, only to find the more experienced Frank Clement in his seat and away before he had realised quite what had happened. Archie was more interested in motorcycle racing than motor cars. Unfortunately, he was killed during practice for the Isle

of Man TT motorcycle races later that year.

From then on Tim Birkin became more and more involved with motor racing, perhaps obsessively so. Late in 1927 he ordered a new 4½-Litre Bentley to full team car specification, and he raced this car extensively throughout the 1928 season. At Brooklands, he led a team of 4½-Litres, finishing third on speed and first in class in the Six Hours Race. Despite tyre failure Birkin, partnered by Jean Chassagne, finished fifth at Le Mans, setting the fastest lap. They lost three hours after a puncture, which resulted in the ruined tyre wrapping itself around the hub/drum assembly and the braking mechanism, followed by the wheel collapsing. At Ards and Boulogne, he finished fifth in the Tourist Trophy and the George Boillot Cup respectively, but in both races finished first on speed.

Autofolio

It was perhaps at the Nürburgring that Birkin conceived his plan to supercharge the 4½-Litre. In the German Grand Prix he was beaten into eighth place by four supercharged SS Mercedes and three Bugattis. The Mercedes were significantly faster than Birkin's standard 4½-Litre. The 7.1-litre SS Mercedes had a power output of some 225 bhp with the supercharger engaged. The blower was driven through a clutch, and brought into operation by flooring the accelerator pedal against a strong spring. They were probably much the same weight as the Bentley, but with a massive power advantage compared to the approximately 130 bhp of the 4½-Litre's engine in racing trim. Whilst a standard 4½-Litre was by contemporary standards a very fast car indeed, in racing form it was being increasingly pressed by the Mercedes and by smaller cars, particularly the Alfa-Romeos. Birkin was intensely patriotic and wished above all else to compete in a suitable British car, and it is reputed that Birkin refused to race an unsupercharged 4¼ Litre again after 1928. On the subject of the Nürburgring race, Birkin merely observed that 'We were hopelessly outclassed'.

Family Tree

The design of the 4½-Litre dates back to 1919, when W.O. Bentley together with F.T. Burgess (of TT Humber fame) and H.F. Varley (ex Vauxhalls) laid down the design of the 3-Litre Bentley. The design of the 4- Litre and hence the Supercharged car was basically an evolution of the earlier car. From an apprenticeship in railway engineering and two years working on Unic taxis, W.O. had run a partnership with his brother, H.M. Bentley, known as Bentley & Bentley, dealing in the DFP car. W.O. rapidly realised the value of racing success from an advertising viewpoint, and took over a 2-litre 12/15 hp car for the purpose. This was fitted with rudimentary coachwork and was extensively 'breathed on'. The limiting factor soon proved to be the pistons, then made either of steel or cast iron, the cast-iron ones tending to crack and the steel ones to break rings. W.O. hit on the idea of using aluminium for pistons, and is generally credited as being the first to do so.

The idea of using aluminium was inspired by a visit by W.O. to the DFP factory. On M. Doriot's desk (DFP stood for Doriot, Flandrin et Parant) was a toy, a miniature piston cast in aluminium, presented to Doriot by their foundry. Although Doriot himself was sceptical, W.O. and the foundry worked out a formula

of 92 per cent aluminium and 8 per cent copper (L8) and cast a set. These were then machined and fitted to the DFP, giving a useful increase in power. They were then lightened still further with no apparent ill effects, and proved to be highly successful. W.O.'s forte, perhaps his genius, was that of the development engineer – extracting the maximum potential from a given design. The 12/40 Speed Model DFP, developed from the ordinary 12/15 car, established innumerable class records in the 1912-1914 era despite stiff competition from Tuck's Humber, which was backed by a large factory.

From the DFP, W.O. worked on aero-engines during the Great War, designing the BR1 and BR2 rotaries, themselves radical redesigns and improvements of the existing Clerget engine, and highly successful in Service use. The success of the BR rotaries gave W.O. the confidence to design his own car from scratch, rather than just continue to sell the products of other firms. W.O. met F.T. Burgess at Humbers where the latter was the Chief Designer, Humbers being heavily involved in manufacturing BR rotaries. Burgess already had a considerable reputation in his own right, having designed the team of Humbers that competed in the 1914 Tourist Trophy race, one of which was driven by Burgess himself in that race. The two discussed a post-war car, Burgess agreeing to leave Humbers and join the embryonic Bentley Motors in January, 1919. W.O., Burgess and H.F. Varley (W.O. readily acknowledged that it was very much a team effort) studied the best of the pre-First World War cars (as there were no new designs available to study in early 1919) to evolve the concept of the 3-Litre as a fast touring car that could be raced.

Drawing on the 1914 Grand Prix Peugeots and Mercedes, the heart of the 3-Litre was its long stroke 4-cylinder engine. Most British engines of the time had long strokes, because the RAC rating that was used for tax purposes was based on the engine bore, but not stroke. The 80x149 mm engine had a capacity of 2996 cc, with non-detachable head (W.O. allocated a very high priority to reliability, and head gaskets were not then noted for their qualities in that area) with four valves per cylinder. The use of four valves gave better cooling, less inertia in the valve train due to lighter valves allowing weaker springs, and less hammering of the valve seats. W.O. had learnt the lesson of good cooling from aero-engine practice. The single overhead camshaft was shaft-driven from the front of the engine by bevel gears, with a cross-shaft gear driving twin magnetos firing two plugs per

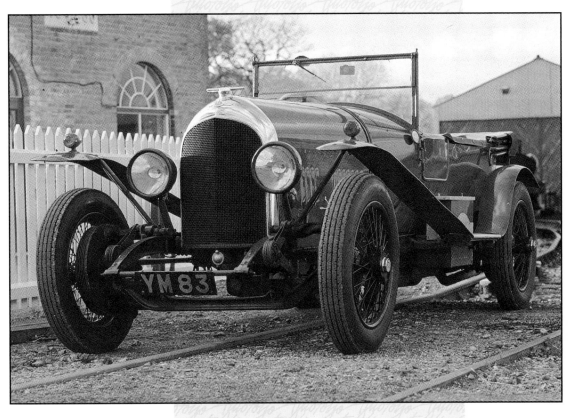

cylinder and a further gear driving the water pump. The overhead camshaft operated the valves through steel rockers, forked for the inlet and two single for the exhaust. The general layout of the top end of the engine is very reminiscent of the highly successful 1914 Grand Prix Mercedes, one of which W.O. had had the chance to inspect when it was recovered from Mercedes' London showroom in Long Acre in 1915

and shipped to Rolls-Royce at Derby.

The bottom end of the engine was basically conventional, the crankshaft running in five main bearings in a cast aluminium crankcase with a cast aluminium sump beneath. The bearing material was

'Bond's car was his only personal hobby. One of the last of the 4½-Litres with the supercharger by Amherst Villiers, he had bought it almost new in 1933 and had kept it in careful storage through the war. It was still serviced every year and, in London, a former Bentley mechanic, who worked in a garage near Bond's Chelsea flat, tended it with jealous care. Bond drove it hard and well and with an almost sensual pleasure. It was a battleship-grey convertible coupé, which really did convert, and it was capable of touring at ninety with thirty miles an hour in reserve'. (*Casino Royale,* Ian Fleming, Jonathan Cape Ltd 1953).

Autofolio

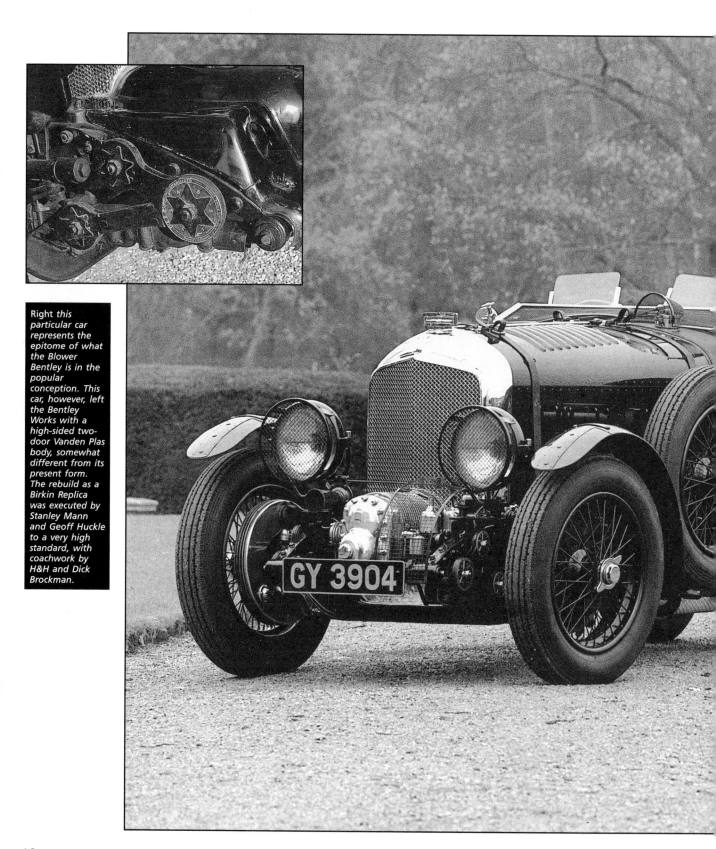

Right *this particular car represents the epitome of what the Blower Bentley is in the popular conception. This car, however, left the Bentley Works with a high-sided two-door Vanden Plas body, somewhat different from its present form. The rebuild as a Birkin Replica was executed by Stanley Mann and Geoff Huckle to a very high standard, with coachwork by H&H and Dick Brockman.*

GY 3904

white metal, cast into the shells and then line bored. The drive was transmitted by a cone clutch to a close ratio 'A' type gearbox, thence by a Bentley-designed pot-joint propeller shaft to the back axle, again of conventional design. The chassis was of basic ladder frame design, with mechanical brakes to the rear wheels and steering by worm and wheel. Suspension was by semi-elliptic leaf springs all round, with friction shock absorbers. The early 3-Litres were all built on a 9 ft 9½ in wheelbase. It has to be remembered that in those days there were virtually no component suppliers, so car manufacturers often had to make virtually everything themselves. The only proprietary items on the Bentley were the expected ones – lamps, wheels, instruments, electrical equipment and the steering wheel.

The chassis were all hand-fitted at Bentley's Cricklewood Works. The manufacturing was all sub-contracted as Bentleys had no in-house facilities, so all casting, forging and machining work was undertaken by outside contractors. The finished parts were then delivered to the Works, where the chassis frames were marked out and drilled by hand before being assembled by a fitter and his mate in the Chassis Shop. Many of the detail parts were hand-fitted and were not interchangeable. Axles were fitted with the chassis upside down, this being returned to the usual orientation to fit the smaller parts. Engines were assembled by a fitter and his mate in the Engine Shop, then run up and checked over on the dynamometer. The engine would then be fitted to its chassis and

Autofolio

fitted with a test rig body in the Running Shop, so that the chassis could be driven and generally checked over. Once passed off it would go to the coachbuilder, for bodywork, wings and suchlike. From there it would return to Cricklewood to be weighed, to ensure that the rear springs were correct for the car weight, and to be checked over before issuing the five-year guarantee that came with virtually all the Vintage Bentley chassis (the Supersports 100 mph chassis only had a one year guarantee). The coachbuilders were issued with drawings to ensure clearances for brake rods, suspension travel, etc, and all these would be checked over before the car was passed off and the guarantee issued. In 1929, the engine build was broken down into stages, more on a production basis, but the cars remained essentially hand-built and individual. That, and the high cost of sub-contract manufacture, made the cars very expensive. Bentleys had only just got their own Machine Shop going just after the time the Blower cars were being manufactured.

Between 1919 and 1927, the 3-Litre acquired brakes to all four wheels, still mechanically operated, but otherwise remained basically unchanged in basic concept. Faster 9 ft Supersports wheelbase chassis were offered, along with the Speed Model on the original 9 ft 9$\frac{1}{2}$ in chassis, and the Long Standard on the 10 ft 10 in chassis for roomier coachwork. The latter used a wider ratio gearbox, the 'B' type, and a lower back-axle ratio. The back-axle was redesigned and improved in 1926, and in the same year the steel rockers were superseded by ones of Duralumin and the one-piece sump replaced the earlier two-piece design.

The 3-Litre was raced extensively, the first major races being at Indianapolis and the Tourist Trophy races in 1922. At Indianapolis the Bentley finished thirteenth, but at the TT on the Isle of Man the three cars finished second, fourth and fifth, winning the Team Prize. At the first Le Mans race, in 1923, a 3-Litre prepared by the Works but entered privately, driven by John Duff and Frank Clement, finished fourth equal, setting the fastest lap. The following year, 1924, Duff and Clement drove another 3-Litre to victory at Le Mans. In 1925, Duff and Woolf Barnato drove a 3-Litre for 24 hours at Montlhéry, averaging 95.03 mph and setting a new world's record. However, in 1925 and 1926, all the Bentleys entered at Le Mans retired, and 1927 started badly with three cars retiring in the Six Hours race (the Birkin car finishing third, as recounted earlier). It was becoming increasingly clear, however, that the 3-Litre was being outpaced in international competition by

such cars as the 3-Litre Sunbeam, fitted with a race-bred twin overhead camshaft engine. A power increase was needed to maintain the Bentley reputation. It has to be remembered that the cars raced by Bentleys were production cars, intended for normal use, whilst those made by other manufacturers were often intended primarily for racing but were also made available to the public.

The 4$\frac{1}{2}$-Litre came about as an evolution of the 3-Litre, to meet this need for more power. The new model was introduced in 1927, on the Long Standard 10 ft 10 in wheelbase 3-Litre chassis as standard; a shorter 9 ft 9$\frac{1}{2}$ in wheelbase variant was available to order. The new engine was of 100x140 mm bore and stroke, otherwise being basically the same as the 3-Litre engine described earlier, using the Duralumin rockers and one-piece sump. The chassis was very similar to the 3-Litre, but with either a 'C' or 'D' type gearbox. The 'C' type gearbox was similar to the 'B' type, but with ratios intermediate to that box and the 'A' type. The 'D' type used the same ratios as the 'A' type, but was of very much more substantial construction. A new proprietary Spicer propeller shaft was fitted. The detail design of the chassis and fittings was very similar to the 3-Litre, but much improved in various respects. Power was up from 85-88 bhp of the Speed Model 3-Litre to 105-110 bhp, with an increase in maximum speed from 85 mph to 92 mph despite the increased weight of the bigger car.

Between 1927 and 1929, the 4$\frac{1}{2}$-Litre was given a single-plate clutch in place of the cone, and semi-servo or 'self-wrapping' front brakes. These had a leading and trailing shoe, and were more powerful than the original twin-leading shoe design. The system was evolved from an idea used on the team cars of reversing the operating levers to the front brakes so that the effect of the front axle winding up on the springs due to torque reaction pushed the brakes on harder. The chassis frame itself was stiffened up after two cars cracked their frames in the 1928 Le Mans race, with various gusset plates added and deeper flanges to the bottom rail. The gauge of the frame was increased from $\frac{5}{32}$ inch to $\frac{3}{16}$ inch. The frames were braced by strut gear, in appearance remarkably similar to that used on locomotives.

The production Supercharged 4$\frac{1}{2}$-Litre was based very heavily on the late 4$\frac{1}{2}$-Litre chassis. The chassis frame was basically the same, apart from a tubular front tie-bar to support the front of the supercharger and a new pressed front cross-member. This supported

the front of the engine, with two circular windows pressed into it for the supercharger trunking on the offside and the controls to the carburettors on the nearside. Heavy pattern bolted strut gear was fitted. The back axle was the same but utilised the differential design of the 6½-Litre. The 6½-Litre differential used the same principles as the 3/4½-Litre unit, but was very much more robustly designed to cope with the increased power. A stronger Spicer propeller shaft with bigger flanges was used, and the 'D' type gearbox.

Steering, suspension and brakes remained the same in outline as the 4½-Litre, with the 'self-wrapping' front brakes. The paper specification of the engine remained much the same, just stronger to take the increased power, with the single plate clutch. In production form power output was 175 bhp, of which approximately 35 bhp was used to drive the supercharger itself. Maximum speed increased from 92 mph of the 4½-Litre to 105 mph.

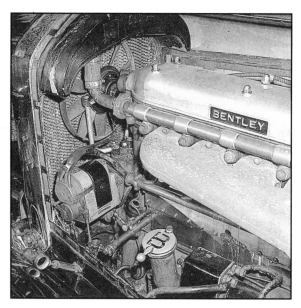

Right *inlet side of the Supercharged engine. The inlet manifold has the large trunking from the supercharger coming in from below, with twin blow-off valves to protect the supercharger in the event of back-firing. Note how complicated the controls are – much more so than on the unsupercharged cars – with the accelerator and hand throttle linkage having to go all the way out to the carburettors at the nearside front of the chassis.*

Above *exhaust side of the Supercharged engine. The co-axial starter motor is not the original, which would have been a Smiths unit, and the electric fan is a modern addition as well. Cooling was always a problem on the Supercharged cars, and the fan is a very sensible provision.*

Concept

Birkins' idea of supercharging the 4½-Litre was a scheme not favoured by W.O. W.O.'s thoughts were very much along the lines of adding litres, a philosophy that he had successfully followed earlier when he had increased the capacity of the 4-cylinder cars from 3-Litres to 4½-Litres. His plan was to follow the same course again, and develop a racing variant of the 6-cylinder 6½-litre car, introduced in 1926 and intended as a town carriage. This car became the Speed Six, which proved to be extremely successful in sports car racing in 1929 and 1930. In the same way that the 4½-Litre succeeded the 3-Litre because the smaller car was no longer competitive, so a successor was now needed for the 4½-Litre with enhanced performance to maintain the Bentley name. The prototype 4½-Litre had set the fastest lap at Le Mans in 1927, before being involved in the pile-up at White House. One of the 3-Litres had gone on to win, despite crash damage to the front end. The 4½-Litre went on to win the 24 Hour Grand Prix de Paris at Montlhéry later in the same year. In 1928, three 4½-Litres finished third, sixth and eighth in the Essex Car Club's Six Hours race, and then first and fifth at Le Mans – despite the leading car's cracking its chassis frame and finishing with no water! Again, as recounted earlier, the Birkin/Chassagne car that finished fifth was delayed by tyre trouble.

In the rest of the 1928 season, however, the 4½-Litres could not manage better than fifth place (Birkin at Ards and Boulogne), and it was clear that a faster car was needed. It was at this point that W.O. and Birkin diverged. Birkin's motives should not be misunderstood. Birkin was not looking for glory for himself in any shape or form. Birkin was intensely patriotic. He wanted to see his countrymen win in British cars and would do anything he could to further that aim. It was his belief that the best way to achieve that was to supercharge the 4½-Litre, and he followed that course with determination without stinting either himself or his own resources.

Because of the shaky finances of the Bentley Company, Birkin was able to pursue his scheme to supercharge the 4½-Litre as a private venture, and then see it taken up as a production proposition. The reason for this was that whilst W.O. Bentley was the Managing Director of the company that bore his name, the purse strings were held by the Chairman, Woolf Barnato. Towards the end of 1925 the Company was virtually bankrupt, in no small part due to the costs of developing the 6½-Litre and putting it into production. Barnato bought his way into the Company in March 1926, and effectively owned it.

Barnato and Birkin were probably the most illustrious of the 'Bentley Boys', the wealthy socialites who drove the green cars to their racing successes. Such was the reputation of the Bentley team that W.O. had his pick of the best amateur sportsmen who were only too happy to accept drives, for which they were, of course, not paid. The 'Bentley Boys' included noted Harley Street physician Dr Dudley Benjafield, the Australian Bernard Rubin who made his money in the pearl trade, Glen Kidston, the Dunfee brothers, Leslie Callingham, Baron d'Erlanger, and the jockey George Duller, as well as professional drivers of the calibre of Frank Clement and Jean Chassagne. Barnato himself inherited a vast amount of money from his father Barney Barnato, who had made his fortune in the South African diamond industry.

Birkin commissioned Amherst Villiers, a talented engineer who had had considerable successes with Raymond May's Brescia Bugattis and then with the Villiers Vauxhall Supercharged Special, a 1922 Tourist Trophy Vauxhall to which Villiers had added a Roots-type supercharger. Several types of supercharger were then available, the Vane and Roots patterns being the most popular.

'I remember a little while ago that a young Cambridge undergraduate came up and confided in me his secret wish to win the Inter-Varsity trials; he said that he had several fast cars, but did not know how to drive them, and wanted my assistance. He was so modest and so obviously keen – I forget if he called me 'Sir' – that I consented to do what I could ... I had the satisfaction of seeing him flushed and excited with victory after his race; and though he was not able to stop at the end and crashed through a fence and a hedge into a field, that lad definitely showed the right spirit. He is now quite a good driver.' (From *Full Throttle',* Birkin, G.T. Foulis & Co, 1932).

The supercharger in all it's glory. The Birkin cars did not have the aluminium shroud fitted to the standard cars, just a wire mesh stoneguard over the carburettors. This is the ribbed pattern unit, as fitted to the second series of 25 of the Supercharged cars. Carburettors are twin SU HVG5s.

WO himself was less than enamoured of the Supercharged car, for many reasons. Perhaps his most telling observation was: 'To supercharge a Bentley engine was to pervert it's design and corrupt it's performance'. W.O.'s viewpoint was possibly jaundiced by having to use the heavier Blower pattern crankshaft on the later, unsupercharged 4½-Litres, which reduced their power output by some 5-10 per cent.

Design

Villiers looked at the Bentley drawings, and realised that extensive redesigning would be necessary to ensure that the engine would be capable of coping with the increased power. First of all he proposed a counter-balanced crankshaft of considerably more massive proportions, with stronger connecting rods and pistons. The crankcase itself was stiffened considerably. Because the main bearing studs went right through the crankcase and bolted the block itself down, the increase in main bearing diameter pushed the studs further apart, necessitating alterations to the cylinder block foot. The main bearing diameter of the crankshaft was increased from 55 mm to 80 mm, with a consequent increase in crankshaft weight from 47 lb to 75 lb. Villiers discussed his proposals with W.O., who was clearly less than happy with the whole scheme. W.O. rejected Villiers' counterbalanced crank, simply making the shaft more massive but without the balance weights. He accepted Villiers' other design changes. There was some talk of a dry-sump lubrication system, but this was not followed up.

There was then the matter of the location of the supercharger. Due to the considerable size of the 4½-Litre engine, there was little room under the bonnet to

Above the exhaust side of the Birkin-type engine; comparisons with the standard car are interesting. Much of Bentley's success in long distance racing was based on meticulous preparation, and although Birkin's team at Welwyn was separate from the Works many of the staff were ex-Bentleys. Note the asbestos lagging on the HT leads, and the larger capacity sump with ribbed sides for better cooling.

Villiers had set himself up as a consultant, working from Piccadilly House, Sackville Street, in London, specifically to assist car manufacturers and related organizations in applying supercharger technology. This was at a time when superchargers were increasingly being used on piston-engined aircraft. Villiers started work on the supercharger installation late in 1928, and it was at this point that the problems started. Villiers needed a set of blueprints for the 4½-Litre engine, which had to be obtained from Bentley Motors. Thus Birkin needed to enlist at least the passive co-operation of the Company. Birkin and Barnato were good friends, so presumably Barnato added his weight to the request. Barnato must have realised that whilst the proposed Supercharged 4½-Litre would be a rival to W.O.'s Speed Six, it gave the Company two avenues of approach, one of which at least was being privately financed. Despite W.O.'s objection to the scheme, Barnato gave it the go-ahead.

fit the supercharger, quite apart from the problem of how it would be driven. W.O. was against chain drive because the chain drives of the time were noisy, and the Bentley literature emphasised the point that everything was positively driven, there being no belts or chains. W.O. would doubtless have wanted to see this practice maintained, with the only available power take-off from the four cylinder engine thus being from the front of the crankshaft. W.O. told Villiers that the supercharger would project in front of the radiator between the dumb-irons, in much the same manner as the dynamo on the 6-cylinder cars. W.O. further told Villiers that there would be no royalty from Bentley Motors, but he would have publicity from Bentley catalogues and the Villiers name on the supercharger itself. Villiers would, of course, have been paid by Birkin. An agreement was drawn up in October, 1928, to the effect that Villiers signed over the use of his patents to Bentleys until May 1929, after which Bentleys would pay a fee to Villiers if they chose to standardise the supercharger.

Villiers went away to work on the supercharger design and installation, between late 1928 and mid-1929. So sure of the outcome were they that Birkin entered two of the cars for the 1929 Le Mans race. The prototype supercharger installation was fitted to Bernard Rubin's own 4½-Litre Le Mans replica YU 3250, with twin Aero Zenith carburettors. Birkin set up his workshops at 19 Broadwater Road, Welwyn Garden City, and took on Clive Gallop to manage and run the project. Unfortunately, Villiers and Gallop did not see eye to eye. Gallop had worked for Peugeots before the First World War, and then flown in the RFC before being taken off flying duties and onto Technical Liaison when it was realised he had an engineering background. After that he had worked on the valve gear of the Experimental 3-Litre Bentleys in 1919 and 1920, before working on the Grand Prix Aston Martins. Gallop subsequently worked for Zborowski at Highbury, preparing and co-driving T.A.D.C. Thistlethwayte's 9 ft chassis 3-Litre Bentley in the 1926 Le Mans race. Birkin had a very high opinion of Gallô, as he liked to be known. Villiers, however, described him as a 'hot air technician', saying that Gallop felt he knew everything and would listen to nobody. This personal dispute possibly ensured the failure of the Blowers before the project even got off the ground.

'I have a vague recollection that we bought a $4\frac{1}{2}$ from which the Blower had been removed; I can visualise it very clearly outside the showroom with the Blower radiator looking very ugly and squat with no Blower in it. The reason for the missing Blower I cannot recall. Blowers in those days were not very popular and were difficult to sell.' Sam Hood, salesman to H.M. Bentley and Partners between 1931 and 1937, in the BDC *'Review'* in 1975.

Villiers stayed long enough to see the first superchargers installed and working. However, it was soon found that there were problems. Villiers' first design had a double-wall casing, cast in aluminium. Inside this ran two involute form rotors, one driven through a flexible coupling (fabric Hardy discs) from the front end of the crankshaft, the other then being driven by a gear train at the front of the supercharger. These then drew mixture from two Zenith carburettors on the nearside, forcing it at pressures up to 12 psi up the trunking to the inlet manifold on the offside of the engine. All very good. The double wall casting was not, however, consistently double skinned along its whole length, and on becoming hot it did not expand linearly. The effect of this was distortion in the casing, resulting in the tips of the rotors touching each other. The superchargers themselves had to be very well made, and David Brown were employed to grind the rotors and gears using the new Swiss MAAG principle. Villiers redesigned the supercharger with the single-wall finned casing, which did have linear expansion properties, and then left the project. On the strength of Villiers' record with Mays' Bugattis and the Villiers Vauxhall it is conceivable that the Blower saga would have been very

much more a success story had he stayed on.

The sting in the tail from W.O.'s point of view was that Bentley Motors had to manufacture 50 production cars, in order to meet the regulations for the Le Mans 24 Hours Race so that Birkin could enter his cars. Birkin's No 1 and No 2 cars (the prototype, YU 3250, was invariably referred to as the No 3 car) were built on chassis numbers HB 3402 and HB 3403. Bentleys sanctioned their cars in batches of 25, the 'HB' series of 4½-Litres running from HB 3401 to HB 3425. Many years later Nobby Clarke, who was then in charge of the Service Department, intimated that the HB was for Henry Birkin and that those 25 cars were to have been supercharged. Presumably there were hold-ups, as they were delivered as standard 4½-Litres, and the first of the production Supercharged cars did not take to the road until October 1929.

Racing

Gallop and his team at Welwyn busied themselves on the No 1 and No 2 cars, and got the No 1 car on the road just days before the 1929 Le Mans race. (Birkin co-drove an unsupercharged 4½-Litre in the Double

Although most of the Blowers delivered were similar to GH 1932, every schoolboy's dream must be the real 'Birkin Blower', the machine of myth and legend. First ingredient in the Birkin recipe is a dashboard with more instruments than many aircraft of the era! The dash itself is of engine-turned aluminium. The engine-turning is done using a hard felt disc impregnated with grinding paste, working in lines across the full width of the dash. Just this operation will take a full day's skilled work.

Twelve race in May, the race that saw the début of the racing variant of the Speed Six. The Speed Six led until the dynamo drive broke up, one of the 4½-Litres finishing second. The 4½-Litre of Birkin/Holder retired with back axle failure.) The No 1 and 2 cars were fitted with identical four-seat touring bodies, made by Harrisons to 'British Flexible' patents. However, errors had been made in the main bearing clearances, and a cold oil pressure of 100 psi dropped almost immediately to nothing. There were also problems with oiling up the plugs. On test at Brooklands, Birkin had endless problems with oiling up, despite trying virtually every type of plug available. The two Blowers had to be scratched from the Le Mans race, and in a rather surprising move Birkin shared the winning Speed Six with Woolf Barnato. Birkin was kept very strictly to team orders, on pain of dire retribution, as W.O. was well aware of his ability to break cars. Bentleys put up two additional 4½-Litres to cover for the missing Blowers, and finished one, two, three, four. The fifth car retired because of magneto problems resulting in cross-shaft gear failure.

Less than a month after the Le Mans race the No 1 car appeared at Brooklands in the Six Hours Race, driven by Birkin. It proved to be significantly faster than the Team 4½-Litres but retired due to an unspecified problem. Such was to be the competition story of the Supercharged cars – fast, but not terribly reliable. Rather like Tim Birkin himself, in fact! It has to be remembered, though, that the development timescale of the Birkin cars was very short, maybe ten months from concept to the production of the first units, and the first race.

By the time of the Irish Grand Prix, held near Dublin on 12 and 13 July, the second of the team cars had been made ready, to be driven by Rubin. Birkin had an extremely fast race with 'Scrap' Thistlethwayte, the latter driving one of the 7-litre supercharged SSK Mercedes, such that the Mercedes retired with a blown gasket. Birkin's car suffered from overheating, and finished third behind Ivanowski's Alfa-Romeo and the Speed Six Bentley of Glen Kidston. Rubin finished eighth. Overheating and lubrication problems dogged the Blowers throughout their racing career. The size of the supercharger reduced the cooling area of the radiator, the core of which was made deeper to counteract this problem. The supercharger also masked off most of the airflow over the sump, resulting in higher oil temperatures. Higher capacity oil pumps and bigger sumps with finned sides were developed to try and lower the oil temperatures. This problem was not

'I did not reach the course until an hour before the start; I was in Le Touquet with Babe Barnato, where he bet me a dinner at the Casino that I would not break the record. I flew to Brooklands, where there was a large crowd, and took the car round once to warm it up. After that I tried never to lift my foot from the accelerator; over the bumpy surface, I was once in the air for forty feet and the car too, but it did two laps of 134.6 and 135.3, and so set up a new record ... I flew back to Le Touquet in the evening and had my dinner with Babe.' Birkin on breaking the Brooklands lap record in the supercharged single-seater, the No. 1 car (*Full Throttle*, Birkin, G.T. Foulis & Co, 1932).

Top *instrumentation on the Team cars was very different from the standard cars. The oversize dinner plate rev counter was to enable the driver to see his revs at a glance; some of the Team Bentleys did not have a speedo at all, others the standard instrument. Note the drip feed for the oil supply to the supercharger gears.*

Left *this view shows the oil tank mounted under the scuttle with the racing quick-release filler above.*

Pre-war quote for removing the Supercharger from a 4½-Litre:
'It must be understood that the Supercharged engine has lower compression, and the connecting rods are heavier, than the standard 4½-Litre and that, therefore, while the maximum speed will only be slightly less, the acceleration will not be so good.

Our charge for removing the Supercharger, supplying and fitting standard SU twin carburettors, induction system and controls, supplying and fitting an adaptor for the crankshaft and steady for the starting handle, together with a special starting handle, would be £45.

The existing radiator would still be used and the cowl at present over the carburettor would have to be modified to fill up the space occupied by the Supercharger. This is a coachbuilder's job, for which there would be a labour charge.

The front road springs would be left as they are, these are actually of a heavier type to suit the extra weight of the Supercharger. If standard front road springs are to be fitted, it necessitates changing the front dumb-irons as well, the charge for this job complete is £11 15s 0d.

All the above prices are quoted on the understanding that the parts removed from the chassis, as a result of the conversion, become our property.'

Autofolio

fully solved until a proper dry sump layout was evolved for the single-seater track car, by which time it was too late anyway.

All three cars (No 1, No 2 and the long chassis prototype car No 3) came to the line for the Tourist Trophy Race at Ards near Belfast in August. Road racing was by then, as now, forbidden on mainland Britain by Act of Parliament, so the Tourist Trophy was run on the Isle of Man and later near Belfast. The Irish Grand Prix, held near Dublin, was started after the Tourist Trophy had moved to Belfast in 1928. Birkin drove the No 1 car, Rubin the No 2 car and Beris Harcourt-Wood, an amateur who lived near Birkin in Norfolk and had become attached to the Birkin team, the No 3 car. After sorting out his insurance, W.O. went along as Birkin's riding mechanic, later recalling the experience as one of the most frightening of his entire life. Shortly after the start of the race, Rubin rolled his car and he

Below the driver's view through the cheese grater! As the twenties progressed the regulations for sports car racing were relaxed, and after 1927 cars no longer had to have hoods at Le Mans. Before then, they had to run for 20 laps with the hoods up, but as speeds increased, this became impractical. Wire mesh superseded glass, and for overtaking on rough circuits the riding mechanic could raise this screen.

and his mechanic were trapped underneath. Fortunately, neither was hurt. Birkin pursued Rudolph Caracciola in the Mercedes, but when the rain came down the latter ran away to a clear win. Birkin finished second on speed but eleventh on handicap, after Harcourt-Wood had retired with engine problems.

The Birkin Cars

	Reg'n	Chassis	Engine	W'base
No 1	UU 5871	HB 3402	SM 3901	10 ft 10 in

Harrison 4-seater then Vanden Plas 2-seater then Thomson & Taylor single-seater

	Reg'n	Chassis	Engine	W'base
No 2	UU 5872	HB 3403	SM 3902	10 ft 10 in 9 ft 9½ in (1930)

Harrison 4-seater then Vanden Plas 4 seater (on 9 ft 9½ in WB)

	Reg'n	Chassis	Engine	W'base
No 3	YU 3250	HB 3404/R	SM 3903	10 ft 10 in

Prototype. Vanden Plas 4-seater.

	Reg'n	Chassis	Engine	W'base
No 4	UR 6571	HR 3976	HR 3976	9 ft 9½ in

New car built 1930. Vanden Plas 4-seater.

	Reg'n	Chassis	Engine	W'base
No 5	UR 9155	HR 3977	HR 3977	10 ft 10 in

Spares car – not raced. VdP 2-seater ex-No 1 car.

The Controversy

Nineteen twenty-nine was the first and last year that Bentley Motors exhibited at the Paris Salon, and the opportunity was taken to announce the introduction of the Supercharged 4½-Litre to the general public. The chassis price was fixed at £1475, £425 more than the standard 4½-Litre but considerably cheaper than the Speed Six at £1800. As with all the Cricklewood Bentleys, the Supercharged car was offered in chassis form only, for the customer to choose his own style of coachwork and coachbuilder. No supercharged cars were ready, though, for Paris, so a standard 4½-Litre Vanden Plas tourer and a Speed Six saloon were exhibited. The Supercharged model was added to the 4½-Litre catalogue, using retouched photographs of the No 3 prototype car YU 3250 as illustration.

The first production car was ready for the Olympia Show held shortly afterwards. Two cars were exhibited, a Vanden Plas tourer on Bentley Motors' stand and a Freestone and Webb fixed-head coupé on Freestone and Webb's own stand. In those days, all the major coachbuilders took stands and displayed their work on whichever chassis they pleased, or chassis from manufacturers with whom they had agreements. The result was that no fewer than five 8-Litre Bentleys appeared at Olympia in 1930. Amherst Villiers took some friends to the Show on the first day, and was shocked to find that his name had been removed from the supercharger casing. The front casting of the supercharger itself had been made with 'Amherst Villiers Supercharger Mk. IV' cast into it in large letters. A small name plate with the Villiers logo was also attached. Bentleys deleted the lettering from the casing, and did not affix the Villiers badge either. The reason for this is obscure. Villiers' account of the events records that his agreement with Bentley Motors stated that his name would appear on the supercharger, and Bentleys had obviously deleted it. This move broke the terms of the October 1928 agreement drawn up between Villiers and Bentley Motors.

> 'By this time [early 1930] Tim Birkin had organised his works at Welwyn Garden City and was assisted by so many enthusiastic experts, amateurs and boffins that I left them to their devices – and was pleasantly suprised to see how magnificently the cars performed even under these adverse circumstances.' Amherst Villiers – with the message written clearly between the lines.

The early superchargers used on the Birkin team cars have the lettering, because the first superchargers were delivered direct to Welwyn from Villiers. The lettering was deleted by Bentleys from the casting patterns as soon as they took them over to make the production units. Admittedly, Villiers' name was more prominent on the supercharger casing than Bentley Motors' own name anywhere else on the car. Whatever the reasons, Villiers sued Bentleys, and tore up the special brochures that he had had printed to give away with the cars. At the ensuing court case, Villiers claimed £1000, but in a deal he claimed was stitched up between Bentley's QC and his, he received £100 on the basis that the rest would be paid later. Villiers did not pursue the matter as vigorously as he perhaps should have done, and never received the rest of the money due to Bentleys' going bankrupt. Villiers claimed that he was not advised by his lawyers that Rolls-Royce had taken over the liabilities of Bentley Motors when they bought the Company in November 1931. Rolls-Royce did not, in fact, take over the liabilities, stating in a rather stuffy letter to a

shareholder that they had taken on the goodwill and all the assets of Bentley Motors but not the liabilities. Villiers did not appear on the list of creditors of the Company in receivership.

Whatever the legal whys and wherefores, Conway, Bentley's head storeman, was sent into the Show on the evening of the first day with the offending plates to affix them to the cars. As most of the cars were delivered with a cowling over the supercharger, the logo was not visible in any case.

This car, PO 3265, chassis SM3902, was Freestone & Webb's exhibit at the 1929 Motor Show with this 'Grafton' fixed-head coupé body. As can be seen, the Villiers name is missing from the supercharger casing. This car was one of two at the Show, and was mentioned in Villiers' injunction taken out against Bentley Motors.

This photograph of YU 3250, the prototype Supercharged car, shows one of the Villiers-made superchargers with his lettering on the casing. It was this photograph, used in Bentley's catalogue with Villiers' name touched out, that fuelled the supercharger controversy.

28

PRODUCTION

Although the list price of the Supercharged car was £1475 for the chassis and £1720 for the Vanden Plas tourer, it seems they were heavily discounted. The new price of MS 3941 with a special Vanden Plas body was £1525 in March, 1931. MS 3932 was taken from Bentley's by Barclays, again with an open Vanden Plas body, and sold to B.W. Preston in May 1931 for £1550. MS 3927 was built up as a stock chassis sent to the Pollen House showroom with a standard Vanden Plas touring body, to be sold by Barclay's in June 1931 for £1395. Another similar car had been sold for £1395 in May. Company figures record that chassis discounts averaged 18 per cent, so despite the Supercharged cars probably being discounted even further, they still didn't sell. Between the Motor Show in October 1930 and January 1931 Bentleys dropped the list price of the chassis from £1475 to £1150, just £100 more than the unblown 4½-Litre, selling at £1050.

Following the Company's demise, prices dropped still further. MS 3938 with a Mayfair open body went from Barclay's to another dealer in November 1931 for £1075, the price including an extra spare wheel, tyre and tube, and a radiator muff. MS 3942 with the same coachwork as MS 3941 was finally sold for £1175 in December 1931 – £350 less nine months later. SM 3915 was next, still a new car, sold again in December for just £950 with a 2/3-seat body by Gurney Nutting. In February 1932, SM 3908 was sold (second-hand) by Barclays to Central Garage in Newcastle-on-Tyne for just £495. In 1950, a similar car was offered for sale by Simmon's of Croydon for £525. £600 for your Blower, squire, and that's my top offer! (Figures courtesy Jack Barclay Ltd, Rolls-Royce and Bentley Dealers, Berkeley Square, London.)

The No.1 Birkin car, UU 5871, at speed in the 1929 Tourist Trophy, fitted with the unlikely-looking Harrison body. This car has one of the four Villiers-made superchargers with the logo on the casing. By the 1930 season all the Birkin cars had new, unmarked blowers. Birkin finished second on speed, but eleventh on handicap.

The first stage of production was the design stage, where the concept was turned into General Arrangement and then detail drawings. In the early stages these would be prefixed 'E' for experimental. Once approved and passed off for production, the General Arrangement drawings acquired an 'A' prefix, and the detail drawings a 'BM' part number. A schedule was then put together, listing all the parts needed to build the complete chassis. As Bentleys was very much an assembly and test organization, the Machine Shops not being put up until after the Blower cars had been built, the drawings would go out to sub-contractors for manufacturing. Stirling Metals did many of the castings, ENV and David Brown various gears and other components, G. Turton Platts forgings. The parts would then come together at Cricklewood stores, managed by Conway, to be issued to the shops to be built up, as detailed earlier.

The first 25 production cars (chassis SM 3901 – SM 3925) used the earlier double-walled plain casing supercharger, which proved to be quite

satisfactory in ordinary use, with twin SU HVG 5 carburettors. The engine had the reinforced crankcase, and a heavier, but not counterbalanced, crankshaft with pistons and connecting rods to suit.The compression ratio was lowered from that of the standard 4½-Litre. In other details, the chassis was basically the same as the standard 4½- Litre. Three Blow-off valves were fitted, one in the trunking by the supercharger and two on the inlet manifold to prevent damage to the supercharger in the event of a backfire. The choke, hand throttle and accelerator controls became something of a nightmare of rods and levers across the front of the engine and out to the carburettors. It was recommended that these were lubricated frequently! The only real changes made during the short production life of the car were the fitting of the ribbed single-wall casing to the second series of 25 chassis (MS 3926 – MS 3950) and the replacing of the standard 4½- Litre 16 gallon tank with the 25

Right close-up of one of the two blow-off valves on the inlet manifold. Note the wire locking of the fixing bolts, another example of the meticulous preparation that went into the Team cars.

gallon 'Tourist Trophy' tank on the last few chassis. Problems seem to have been confined to a tendency to run hot in traffic (due to the smaller, thicker radiator) and a tendency to pinking, even on 50/50 benzole and petrol. That was solved by a further drop in compression ratio. Most of the cars were delivered with a compression ratio of 5.0:1, but some of the

This view is from underneath the front of the car, showing the first of the three blow-off valves mounted in the trunking on the off-side of the Blower. These have a spring-loaded valve that comes off it's seating in the event of a backfire to prevent damage to the supercharger.

later cars were dropped to 4.5 to 1 by fitting a compression plate between the cylinder block and the crankcase. Most of the early chassis had their pistons changed, the later design intended presumably to reduce further the tendency to pinking. In cold weather the carburettors can ice up, a tendency probably reduced by the aluminium cowl.

Commercially, the Supercharged cars proved unsuccessful. Despite the glamorous image of Tim Birkin and his stable, customers simply did not line up to pay large amounts of money for what was basically a 1919 design, itself based on 1914 concepts, updated and redesigned. Unfortunately, by the time the Supercharged car was introduced late in 1929, after the Wall Street crash, sales of all models of Bentley cars were falling off as the Depression started. It is conceivable that wealthy customers might have been put off by the slightly 'new fangled' nature of the supercharger itself, and the racy, even *outré*, air of the Blower cars in a more class conscious society. Between October 1929 and July 1931 maybe 40 of the Supercharged cars were sold, compared to maybe

80 Speed Sixes in the same 21 month period. In total, 182 Speed Sixes were sold between October 1928 and July 1931, which gives some idea of the effects of the Wall Street crash on luxury car sales.

That Bentley Motors produced the absolute minimum number of cars to meet the Le Mans regulations is confirmed by the engine number series. Production was sanctioned in batches of 25, but due to testbed requirements they always used more engines than chassis. Thus, for the 8-Litre they had to start another series of 25 numbers to build enough engines for the 100 chassis built. The 8-Litres ran in four series, prefixed YF, YR, YM and YX. The fifth series was prefixed YH. Similarly, for the $4\frac{1}{2}$-Litre two series of 25 chassis were built, VF and VA, with VP started for the additional engines needed. For the Blowers, Bentleys extended the numbers of the MS series to MS 3953 instead of ending at MS 3950, rather than start a new series of numbers. This indicates strongly that there

In 1930, the Supercharged $4\frac{1}{2}$-Litre chassis was priced at £1475, or £1720 for the complete open touring car. Only eight more expensive chassis were available, two of which were also Bentley products (the $6\frac{1}{2}$ and 8-Litres). Four-cylinder cars comprised only just over 20 per cent of the cars available, cars with fixed cylinder heads less than 10 per cent. ('Autocar' figures).

was no intention whatsoever to start a new series of chassis, which would have been had there been a demand from Sales. Of the 50 cars, all but six were fitted with open coachwork, mostly taking the form of standard Vanden Plas four seaters (Vanden Plas had very close links with Bentley Motors, and bodied virtually all the team cars). The 4-cylinder Bentley chassis were not really suitable for closed coachwork, especially the metal-roofed variety, which often suffered from drumming. All of the six chassis fitted with closed coachwork have either disappeared or been rebodied as tourers.

Above *the Blower at rest. The extended bonnet, some 9 inches longer than standard, was a common feature. Originally intended for racing, to give better access to the under-scuttle area, it was adopted by coachbuilders as a styling trick to give the impression of a bigger and more impressive engine.*

Left *Close-up of the Vanden Plas door-plate. The 'B' was cut out and stuck onto the door panel before sticking on the leather.*

Autofolio

THE SUPERCHARGED 4½ LITRE MODEL

Designed for the super-sporting enthusiast

AS the result of experiments extending over a long period the Company has decided to produce a super-charged edition of the famous 4½ Litre Model. The additional unit obviously enhances the car's performance but this is of such a high standard on the ordinary chassis, that the appeal of the new type will be to the super-sporting enthusiast whose delight it is to possess just that "little bit extra."

The engine has of course been altered in many respects in order to deal reliably with the increased power provided.

The crankshaft is of a new and heavier design and the crankcase has been strengthened. A different type of camshaft is employed while special con rods giving greater strength are adopted with special pistons designed to dispense the extra heat necessarily generated.

The drive of the supercharger is taken from the front of the crankshaft through fabric joints to one shaft of a twin-rotor Roots-type Blower which is fitted in an aluminium casing between the front dumb irons below the radiator, which has been redesigned for the purpose.

The super-charger is arranged so that the lubrication system of the engine feeds the gear wheels which drive one rotor shaft from the other and also supplies enough for the rotor blades themselves.

Two carburettors are fitted on one side of the casing through which the super-charger obtains mixture and expels it on the other side under pressure to a pipe carried right up to the intake ports of the cylinder block. A series of spring loaded safety valves are arranged in the inlet pipes in order to safeguard it and the supercharger should a blow back occur.

Twin S.U. Carburettors are employed, a Revolution Counter is included, and 33 × 6.00 tyres are fitted. The back axle ratios are 3.3 to 1 or 3.53 to 1.

In other respects the specification is the same as that of the Standard 4½ Chassis on page 14.

In accordance with usual Bentley policy this model has been tested in road races during 1929, and as results show, has proved to be highly satisfactory.

The supercharger is the "Amherst Villiers Mark IV."

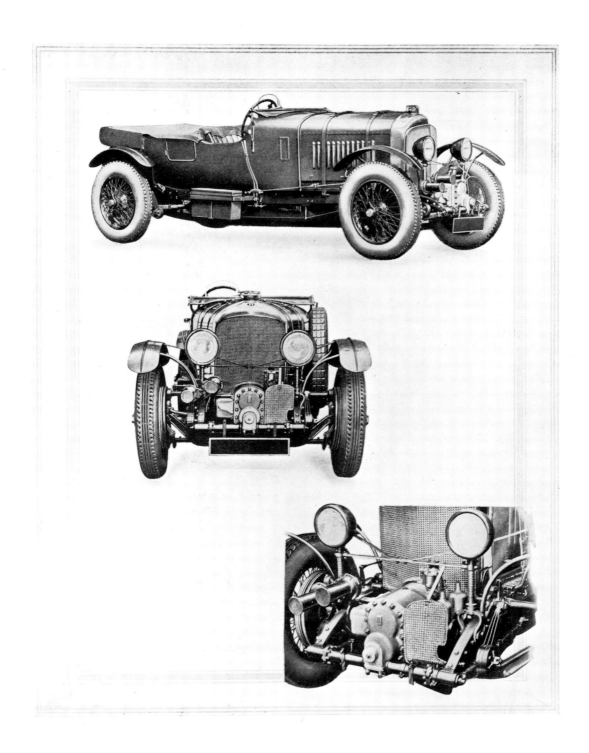

Historical Persepective

The overall reaction from the motoring press of the time was perhaps restrained, but generally complimentary. It was generally agreed that the car was a true 100 mph car, with exceptionally good performance, and that that performance had been obtained without making the car in any way temperamental. *Motorsport* commented in their road test of January 1931 that: 'The supercharging has made possible remarkable acceleration, and when a stretch of open road appears, and the gears are used as they should be, the car momentarily doffs it's sheeps clothing and reveals its ancestry of well-tried racers', concluding by saying: 'In short, the 4½-Litre Supercharged Bentley is a car for the connoisseur of sporting cars, and moreover, proof that this country can still make a car which can compete with confidence and success with the best the world produces.'

The Motor started their report of 22nd April 1930 with: 'The recipe is as follows – Take a sturdy chassis, install an engine rated at 25 hp, add a supercharger, fit an open body, wings and windscreen, and make the complete vehicle have a speed range from 9 mph to 103 mph on top gear. Do all these things and you will have arrived about half way towards the achievement that the 4½-Litre Bentley represents.' The report goes on to praise the performance and quiet running of the car, commenting that 'we obtained a series of braking figures which were so good as to make us recheck them lest a mistake should have occurred!' From 50 mph, they reckoned that the car could be stopped in just 80 feet. 'Summing up, this 4½-Litre Supercharged Bentley can be reported a great success, and is undoubtedly a car which will add still further lustre to the name and fame of the makers'.

The Autocar's report of 19th September 1930 reads in similar style, headed 'The appeal of immense power linked with great docility' and ending 'A car with the strongest possible individuality, and it is certain that it is immensely likeable no matter from what angle one may regard it'. The overwhelming impression received now from reading contemporary road tests is that all agreed that it was a very good car, but that somehow it was not quite the scintillating experience that might have been expected on taking to the road in one of the fastest road-going production sports car from a firm with the reputation in motor racing that Bentley's then had.

In terms of contemporary cars, it is difficult to find any that can be considered as competitors to the Supercharged 4½-Litre. Bugatti and Alfa-Romeo both had the outright performance, but neither fit the bill of a full, four-seat touring car, or were really suitable for closed coachwork. Perhaps only Mercedes can be compared, with the formidable SS and SSK sports cars, as Teutonic in their styling as the Bentley was quintessentially British. The Mercedes, however, lacked the stamina of the Bentley, and owners were advised not to use the clutch-operated supercharger for more than very short periods because of the risk of damage to the engine. The concept of the Mercedes was different from that of the Bentley. The Bentley was essentially a touring car with the supercharger added to enhance the general performance of the car, the supercharger being driven the whole time. Apart from a gentle whistling noise from air being sucked through the carburettors, the supercharger is unobtrusive in operation. The same cannot be said for the Mercedes, which produced a noise that has been compared to a stuck pig. The Mercedes supercharger was intended only to provide staggering acceleration, by flooring the accelerator to engage it via a clutch. Otherwise, the car behaves as a normally aspirated car, but still with formidable performance. The supercharger was intended to be used for periods of not more than 15 seconds. The difference between the Bentley and the Mercedes is shown by the carburettor arrangements. The Bentley supercharger draws mixture through the carburettors and then compresses it, while the Mercedes supercharger blows through the carburettors, hence the need for full throttle before engaging the blower.

Perhaps no other manufacturer offered the same standards of performance and comfort in such a usable form as the Supercharged Bentley. Equally, the fact that nobody else did, perhaps indicates that there was no real demand for such a motor car.

More Racing

The last major race of 1929 was the 500 Miles Race, held at Brooklands. This was for stripped racing cars, and was for some years the fastest motor race in the world. Average speeds were higher than even those at Indianapolis. Birkin had had the No 1 car rebodied by Vanden Plas with a very light shell-type body, not

This very attractive drop-head coupé by Gurney Nutting is very much an early thirties design, and shows how dated the Vanden Plas body shown on GH 1932 was becoming. This car is chassis MS 3931, registered FS 1179, delivered to James Bryson.

The No.1 Birkin car with two-seat Vanden Plas coachwork in the 1929 500 Miles Race at Brooklands. On the banking, this car, with Birkin driving, would have been doing about 130 mph. Birkin later retired due to the exhaust's disintegrating and setting fire to the body.

much wider than a single-seater, with an outside exhaust. W.O. advised Birkin before the start of the race that the exhaust system would break up under racing conditions, which it did, setting fire to the body and forcing Birkin to retire after 420 miles.

Birkin had set up his Works at Welwyn Garden City as quite a little factory, employing some 30 people and offering expertise and consultancy services to the motor industry. Whether they did any work for anyone else is not clear, as they seem to have been fully occupied running the team of Supercharged cars. They did maintain quite a few Bentleys for private owners, several of which were rebuilt to team specification and raced by their owners. All in all the exercise must have cost Birkin a great deal of money, which he could not provide indefinitely. The need for more cash was met by the Hon. Dorothy Paget, Lord Queenborough's daughter, whom Birkin had wooed away from her earlier love of horse racing.

She reputedly had a private income of £100,000 a year, a vast sum by any standards, and agreed to sponsor Birkin's motor racing aspirations. It is an interesting parallel that both Tim Birkin and Bentley Motors were bailed out of their financial difficulties by wealthy patrons, Woolf Barnato and Dorothy Paget respectively, and that both then went under when that patronage was removed.

The immediate result of this was the rebuilding of the No 1 car, UU 5871, as a single seat track car, with coachwork by Thomson & Taylors at Brooklands. The No 2 car UU 5872 was rebuilt on a short chassis frame, and a new car referred to as the No 4 car registered UR 6571 was built up as a sister car, also on a 9 ft 9½ in frame. The chassis frames were obtained by Gallop from Mechans of Glasgow who made all the Bentley frames, but the Birkin frames were assembled with fitted bolts rather than rivets. Bentleys allowed Birkin to build up to 25 cars, allocating chassis numbers HR 3976 – HR 3400. The No 4 car was numbered HR 3976. It is clear that there was a high degree of co-operation between Bentleys and Birkin, despite W.O.'s misgivings. As the public saw the Birkin cars as Bentleys, it was of course important from the Company's viewpoint that the Birkin cars were seen to be successful, as although they were entirely separate their performance inevitably reflected on the parent concern. Gallop later admitted that they added a lot of weight to the Supercharged cars with fittings and detail work, which was a handicap. The new No 4 car was fitted with the Paget crest between the radiator cap and the Bentley badge in acknowledgement of Dorothy Paget's sponsorship. The single-seater was on test at Brooklands by March 1930, and in the Easter Monday meeting broke the lap record no less than four times, finally setting it at 135.33 mph.

All three of the road cars, YU 3250, UU 5872 and the new car UR 6571 were entered for the Double Twelve race at Brooklands on the 9th/10th May 1930. The Double Twelve, run by the Junior Car Club, was an attempt to emulate Le Mans, but run in two twelve hour stints from 8 am to 8 pm over two days, because night driving was not allowed at Brooklands. The track was very close to Weybridge, and the residents objected to the noise. After the first lap the six Bentleys entered occupied the first six places, Birkin lapping in the early stages at over 97 mph. However, Jack Dunfee retired YU 3250 at 3.30 pm with a broken valve, and Birkin retired UU 5872 an hour later with a cracked chassis frame, probably caused by

In 1932, at full throttle the single-seater consumed fuel at the rate of one gallon every 73 seconds. A change to a pair of 62 mm downdraught SU carburettors reduced that figure to 59 seconds, or barely 2 mpg at racing speeds.

'I really think that ... Birkin was the best driver of the lot. He would class with Jim Clark ... or Stirling Moss.' (Wally Hassan) 'When he approached a corner he would throw the handbrake on, and then carry on with his braking and gear-changing, heel-and-toe on the flat pedals; get into gear all ready and then throw the handbrake off, after the corner. He was the only one that ever used to do that. He was a marvellous driver – there's no question of it – really terrifically fast – no nerves at all.' [Leslie Pennal]. (From *The Other Bentley Boys*, Elizabeth Nagle, Harrap & Co. 1964. Hassan and Pennal were racing mechanics with Bentleys).

hitting the kerb at high speed. Benjafield retired the last Blower, UR 6571, early on the second day with back-axle problems. The story goes that he pushed the car half way around the track and dismantled the back-axle to reveal a damaged pinion. The Works Speed Six Bentleys finished first and second.

The same three cars were entered for the Le Mans race six weeks later on 21st/22nd June. 'For many weeks they [Caracciola and Le Mans] had been in my own mind, coupled, like Calais with Philip on Mary Stuart's heart, a place with a name, Le Mans with Caracciola.' (from Birkin's Autobiography, *Full Throttle*). However, the Blower team had their problems. The cars overheated on the French petrol, so the compression ratios were raised by removing the compression plate and running on pure benzole. However, the long chassis car YU 3250 did not start. Between Wednesday and Sunday Birkin's mechanics got only 10 hours' sleep. It was only through the co-operation of a local garage that the other two

Autofolio

Supercharged cars started at all. Birkin set the fastest lap at 89.69 mph, chasing Caracciola's Mercedes, passing him at about 125 mph on the run down to Mulsanne, despite a stripped tread on one of the rear tyres. Because of the weight of the Supercharged cars, their high centre of gravity and the heat of the day, the Dunlop racing covers developed a tendency to throw treads, to the great discomfiture of the Dunlop reps who were present. The Team Speed Sixes had the same problem but to a lesser extent. The Mercedes did not suffer at all although they were also using Dunlops. The Birkin/Chassagne car, however, retired after 138 laps with a broken con rod. The Benjafield/Ramponi car covered six more laps before retiring with a collapsed piston. Although one of the Works Speed Sixes crashed, the other two finished first and second.

Shortly after the Le Mans race, Bentley Motors retired from racing. Their retirement was prompted by several factors; partly because it was difficult to improve on the success they had already achieved, but probably mainly for financial reasons. Quite simply, the parent company was in increasingly dire financial straits. The Birkin équipe was not affected by Bentley's retirement, appearing in force at the Irish Grand Prix at Dublin on the 19th July. All three road cars were entered, the long chassis car driven by Beris Harcourt-Wood, and the short cars by Birkin and Chassagne. The race was run over 70 laps, the three Mercedes giving the three Bentleys two laps on handicap. However, two of the Bentleys (Harcourt-Wood and Chassagne) had lubrication system problems in practice. In the race, Birkin and Caracciola set a terrific pace, Caracciola passing Birkin to recover one of his credit laps after 34 of the 70 laps. It was to be a close race! Unfortunately, the lubrication problems that dogged the other cars caught up with Birkin, who had first to change a broken oil pipe and then stop again to work on the engine, with the car smothered in oil. All this dropped the Bentley back to fourth place – the other two cars were unplaced.

The three road cars were entered again for the Tourist Trophy race near Belfast, five weeks after the Grand Prix on 23rd August. Birkin was increasingly under pressure to produce some results (to justify his sponsorship) – Dorothy Paget had already hinted that she would not extend her sponsorship to a second season. So far, the Bentleys and Mercedes had met three times, and the score was two to Mercedes and one to Bentley (a Works Speed Six, not a Blower). The

Alfa-Romeos were also proving to be very fast. The short cars were driven by Birkin, with Benjafield and Chassagne sharing the other. Bertie Kensington-Moir drove the long car, as Harcourt-Wood was ill. Three Mercedes were entered, but Caracciola was disqualified because his car had a larger supercharger then standard (the so-called 'elephant' blower). The 1750 cc Alfa-Romeos proved to be exceptionally fast (the race was run on handicap) and the larger cars were well back in the running. Birkin's race ended abruptly, when his attention was distracted by his riding mechanic, Whitlock, looking down at the floor. Birkin found himself wrongly placed, and spun round, hitting a telegraph pole and then demolishing a low wall at Ballystockart. Kensington-Moir finished eleventh, and the other car only covered 27 of the 30 laps in the allotted time. The Alfas finished first, second and third. In September, Birkin entered one of the short chassis road cars (UR 6571) for the French Grand Prix at Pau. Due to poor regulations, based on a fuel consumption formula, Grand Prix racing was in decline, so the race was run as 'Formula Libre'. Birkin's Bentley weighed some two tons to the 1 ton of the Bugattis and Delages, but top speeds were similar, of the order of 135 mph. It was a thrilling race, Birkin driving on top form. On the straights, he was just about able to claw back losses on the windy bits. Birkin gradually moved up the field, just missing the limp body of Sabipa, one of the Bugatti drivers, thrown from his car across the track. Birkin worked up to second place, 3 minutes 26 seconds after 'Phi-Phi' Etancelin's Bugatti, having averaged 88.5 mph for the 245 miles. Etancelin had missed his pit stop because of the proximity of the Bentley, and was virtually out of fuel with five of the six clutch retaining bolts broken. It was the finest performance from the Blower cars.

The Birkin team appeared together just once more, in the 500 Miles Race in October, over the Outer Circuit at Brooklands. The two short cars were driven by Eyston/Harcourt-Wood and Hall/Benjafield. Birkin and Duller drove the single-seater. Eyston and Harcourt-Wood retired one of the short cars with magneto drive failure; the single-seater suffered from misfiring and was not running to form, sounding like a motorcycle. Eddy Hall and Benjafield lapped steadily at over 120 mph, chasing the 750 cc Austin Sevens that were leading on handicap. Despite averaging over 112 mph, the Hall/Benjafield Bentley could only manage second place to the Austin Seven of Sammy Davis and the Earl of March. It was to be the swansong of

the Blower team.

By the end of 1930, Dorothy Paget's patience with the Birkin team had evidently run out, and she cut off the money supply. Under the circumstances there was little that Birkin could do, as Birkin & Coupers did not generate enough money to support a full four-car team racing internationally. A set of spare parts was built up into a No 5 car UR 9155, chassis HR 3977, which was then sold, presumably to raise some money. Couper always maintained that he was 'done' by Birkin, but he did at least get some good cars to drive! All the team cars were advertised for sale in *Motorsport* of May 1931, but in the end Dorothy Paget retained the single-seater until 1939, allowing Birkin to race it at Brooklands. Birkin himself was obviously somewhat embittered by the lack of a competitive British car. Subsequently he won the 1931 Le Mans race in a Maserati partnered by Lord Howe. Birkin was even urther mortified to receive a telegram from Mussolini congratulating him on his win 'for Italy!'

Two Supercharged cars were exhibited at the 1930 Olympia Show, both fitted with Vanden Plas coachwork. Bentley Motors exhibited a high-sided two-door, four-seat open tourer, a transitional style of coachwork from the fabric bodies of the twenties to the more curvaceous metal panelled styles of the thirties. Vanden Plas themselves exhibited a fixed-head coupé body on a Supercharged chassis. The chassis price remained at £1475. By January 1931, however, the chassis price was dropped to £1150, the four-seater tourer coming down from £1720 to £1395 and the sporting two-seater from £1840 to £1515.

The End

In July 1931, Bentley Motors themselves went into receivership when Woolf Barnato refused to put up any more money. The Company had been hit by falling sales, and was heavily in debt. After several months of negotiations with Napiers, in a surprise move the Company was taken over by Rolls-Royce. Almost immediately they shut down the Cricklewood Works, and the remaining unsold chassis were disposed of to Jack Barclays. Among these were several Supercharged cars, seven of the last eight cars being fitted with drophead coupé coachwork to order by Vanden Plas for Barclays. They were all eventually sold, but not until well into 1932. Rolls-Royce dropped all the old Bentley models, producing the new 3½- Litre Derby Bentley in

The trouble with the super-chargers', recalled Nobby Clarke (manager of Bentley Motors Service Department) 'was that we knew nothing about them at the time. Nothing about the effect of pressures, or the effect of overloading – all the problems related to them … I was against the idea right from the start, and for the first and last time I swore at W.O. over those damn Blowers. You see, being up at Service and away from the Works at the time, I didn't know what he thought of them, and naturally, as they were going ahead, I assumed he was in favour … One of the main troubles of the superchargers was the effect on plugs: they could not keep a plug in the damn things. A Blower eats plugs like a donkey eats hay … No, those superchargers were a very bad idea, and they did us a lot of harm.'
(From *The Other Bentley Boys*, Elizabeth Nagle, Harrap & Co. 1964).

1933. They did experiment with a supercharger, but decided that it was not really a practical proposition.

Postscript

Birkin continued to race the single-seater until his untimely death, finally setting the Brooklands lap record at 137.96 mph. Only two cars ever officially lapped Brooklands faster, the Barnato-Hassan at 142.6 mph and the Napier-Railton at 143.11 mph. Both were highly specialised track racing cars, unlike the Birkin car which was still close to a production car. Birkin died of blood poisoning in 1933, a legacy of malaria caught in Palestine during the First World War. Birkin's last two years were unhappy. Bentley's retirement and the failure of the Blowers left him no choice but to race Italian cars, then the death of his father in 1931 and the unfortunate partnership with Mike Couper plunged him into fits of depression. The No 4 car was sold to France, and was raced at Le Mans in 1932 by 'Mary' (Pierre Brousselet) and J. Trevoux, lasting seven laps, and again by Trevoux and Gas in 1933, crashing on the first lap. R. Murton-Neale raced the long chassis No 3 car at Brooklands. The identities of the Birkin cars remained a mystery for some years, as the long chassis car was sold with a different registration plate (JH 3115 in place of YU 3250) and the Nos 2 and 4 cars were sold with registration plates exchanged. The single-seater was reregistered NUL 618 after the war. Its original number UU 5871 was finally tracked down on a milk float in Ireland!

Vintage Bentleys descended into the doldrums in the thirties, in no small part because of high road tax, but virtually none of the Supercharged cars were broken up or scrapped. At least four cars, however, were converted to unsupercharged 4½-Litres before the Second World War. It would seem that even then the Supercharged cars possessed a certain cachet among connoisseurs. After the war vintage Bentleys enjoyed a resurgence, not least because they were still competitive in club racing. Alick Pitts was a well-known competitor at the Brighton Speed Trials and other venues in the No 5 car UR 9155, and when the long chassis car YU 3250 was rebuilt by Harry Rose in the 1960s it was found to be still capable of speeds of over 120 mph. Something of a fashion then developed for rebuilding Supercharged cars as Birkin team car replicas, many of these by Townshend's Elmdown Engineering. The value of the Supercharged cars gradually rose, and the Vintage car movement was shaken when £20,000 was paid for an Elmdown Birkin replica at auction in 1972. From then on, the Supercharged cars have risen rapidly and dramatically in value. This increase is a reflection of the perceived desirability of the Supercharged car, which has been described as a triumph of form over function. Much of their appeal, as with all the Vintage Bentleys, is that the cars have more than adequate performance to keep up with modern traffic and are generally very reliable. Of the 50 production cars, just over 40 survive. The cars were very thoroughly researched by Stanley Sedgwick, then President of the Bentley Drivers' Club, in 1973. However, there is a firm in the North of England making complete new Blower units, and several 4½-Litres have been or are being converted to Supercharged cars. It will not be long before there are more Supercharged cars in existence than were built by Bentley Motors!

Several possible candidates were considered for comparison purposes with the Blower, but in the end a 3-Litre Bentley was chosen. The 3-Litre enjoyed the same sort of performance advantage when it was new in the early twenties that the Blower enjoyed at the end of that decade. It is also neatly sandwiched between the pre-First World War 4-cylinder racing cars and the Blower car, which represents the last of the dinosaurs, the big 4-cylinder cars.

The next problem – to find two suitable cars! First of all, it was felt desirable to choose two cars that are as original as possible, partly because well-worn Bentleys generally drive better than tight, newly-restored ones. The other factor is that, as virtually all sixty-year-old cars have been rebuilt, sometimes several times, it is debatable how typical of the model when new any particular car is. It would be difficult to choose two more original cars than Tim Scott's Supercharged 4½-Litre and Ted Parkinson's 3-Litre. Both cars are fitted with Vanden Plas four-seater coachwork to Bentley Motors' instructions, bodies which are still fitted and still in very original order. Both cars were rather special when new, and still retain that patina that a rebuilt car can only aspire to. Understandably, it was with some trepidation that I approached both these irreplaceable cars, bearing in mind the gearbox's reputation as one of the most difficult fitted to any Vintage car!

First of all, one has to forget any analogy with modern motor cars – apart from the obvious, the experience is quite different. Taking the 3-Litre first, one gets into the car through the tiny door on the nearside – only two doors are provided to retain rigidity in the coachwork, which is an ash frame skinned in aluminium. There is no driver's door on the offside, as the gear and brake levers make such an arrangement impractical. One has to slide into place across the passenger seat into the driver's seat. Similarly, the back seat passengers are served by a door on the offside. It is quite a step up, the driving position being rather lofty. The driver sits with his head some five feet off the ground. This does give a very good view, over the roofs of the modern cars. The seats are of the bucket variety, and really rather comfortable, but are definitely not made for those of ample proportions. It is possible to climb in from the offside, but it is difficult to do this with dignity! Once seated, the driving position is dominated by the 16 inch corded steering wheel (in those days, boy racers fitted *larger* wheels, not smaller ones). One sits close up to the wheel, with the side of the body very close, for the coachwork is really rather narrow. In front, the pedals are not what might be expected – the massive clutch and brake pedals are positioned on each side of the central accelerator, which is just a diminutive brass button. The gearlever falls well to hand on the right hand side (on this

3-Litre, it has been lengthened and cranked slightly backwards), and the long handbrake is situated outside the body.

The dashboard has all the controls usual to a car of this period, with, most importantly, the hand pump for the pressurised fuel feed with it's pressure gauge, and the oil pressure gauge. The layout is Smith's bezel-wind 8-day clock on the far left, then the AT speedo and rev counter well over to the nearside, the Smith's starter button located in between them. A pull-out dashlamp and 0-5 psi pressure gauge for the petrol pump are followed by the pump itself, then another pull-out dashlamp and the bezel switch/ammeter. The latter is another Smith's instrument, consisting of a centre-zero ammeter contained in a casing, the rim of which rotates to operate the lights. The legend 'Off – Sides – All On' is displayed in a little window. Next is the Bentley Motors switchplate, engraved with the chassis number and fitted with separate switches for the two magnetos and the dynamo. In the centre of the switchplate is the knurled knob for the choke. Finally, on the right, a dash lamp and matching Smith's water temperature and oil pressure gauges. In so far as Vanden Plas had a standard dashboard layout, this one is fairly close to it, but has rather more instruments than the usual Speed Models, many of which were not fitted with rev counters. On this occasion the instruments generally speaking did not get much

Below *general view of the 3-Litre engine. Visible is the massive flywheel with its starter ring gear on the left, and the ML CG4 magneto to the right. In the early part of this century, magnetos were almost universal, coil ignition tending to take over in the thirties.*

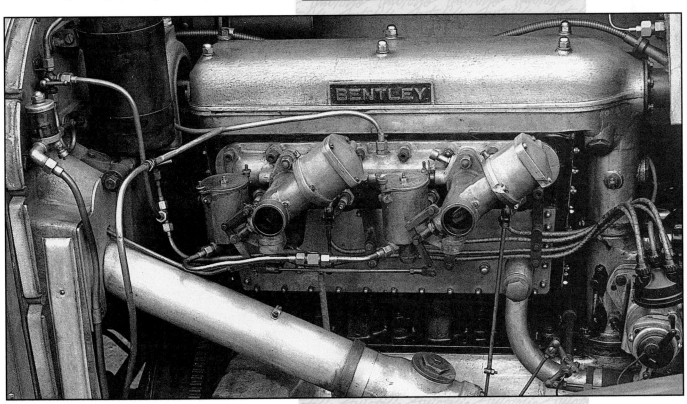

attention – I was far too busy concentrating on other things!

To start, after checking for neutral, one retards the ignition lever on the top of the steering column and opens the hand throttle. The pressure feed for the tank has to be pumped to about 1½ psi, the twin magneto switches on the engraved switchplate are pressed in, and firm pressure on the mushroom-shaped Smith's starter button results in the classic Bentley burble. To get away, advance the ignition, dip the clutch, engage first, release the handbrake and gently let the clutch in. The cone clutch on this car is very sweet in operation. To try to prevent dental grinding noises, the changes up the box are double-declutched: depress the clutch pedal – move the gear lever into neutral – release the clutch pedal momentarily – depress the clutch pedal – engage the higher gear and release the clutch. So far, so good – but the gearbox is quite, quite different from any modern one. Firstly there is no slop in the linkage, which is solid to the selectors itself, so the feel is marvellous. However, there is no syncromesh, so the

changes have to be exactly timed. This 3-Litre has a properly set up clutch stop, and the change is comparatively easy. My initial attempts were not too awful, and improved later after a brief instruction from Ted. Basically, you have to use your ears to establish a set of reference points, from which, with experience, you can play tunes up and down the box. The feeling of a slick, silent change is very satisfying!

The steering is high geared and very positive, with lots of feel. The earlier 3-Litres with the high-geared steering, longer drop arm and beaded edge tyres must have had marvellous steering – light and incredibly direct. The 3-Litre gets away very well, the engine feeling as if it could go on and on – if there were room on these Isle of Wight roads. It is a very willing engine, which responds to hard driving. It is, in fact, a suprisingly easy car to drive – until the time comes to change down. Again, one has to double-declutch, at which point an urgent need is felt for an additional foot. Basically, one is trying to operate the clutch, brake, move the gear lever, steer, and blip the throttle to rev up the gearbox internals, simultaneously. With practice all of this can be accomplished smoothly, but to the novice Bentley driver, the initial prospect is rather daunting! No wonder many of the team drivers used to throw the handbrake on before corners, do everything required, and then throw it off on the exit! I would have to admit, in the past, to having coasted into junctions in neutral, having completely lost it. The obvious solution would be to learn how to heel-and-toe. The brakes are rather non-standard in that a servo has been added. The pedal travel was rather excessive, Ted commenting that it needed taking up (the mechanical brakes have a single-point take up for the footbrake under the floor on the driver's side of the car). The brakes were good, but I did find the long travel not very reassuring.

Having come to terms with the gearbox, the car is great fun. It is light, with delightful steering, good performance, and a lovely view down the hock bottle shoulders of the bonnet and the blade wings framing the Smith's lamps. The only thing one has to remember is to keep the pressure up in the tank, using the dashboard mounted pressure pump. That pump must have been hard work during the 24 hour races at Le Mans.

Getting out of the 3-Litre and straight into the Supercharged 4½-Litre made the comparison even more interesting. The driving position of the Blower car is similar, but the cockpit is noticeably wider, with more elbow room. The seats are more touring, wider and with more padding. The wheel is similarly close up, and of the same size as the 3-Litre, but has not been corded. Instrumentation again is similar, but with Jaeger speedo and rev counter. The arrangement here is Ki-Gass (used to inject neat petrol into the inlet manifold for starting) and two switches for the petrol pumps, Jaeger speedo, Hobson telegauge (petrol gauge), and Jaeger rev counter. Next are two non-functioning switches, together with the Smith's starter button and a pull-out dashlamp, then a replacement ammeter in a later switchplate. Then the usual Bentley switchplate, followed by the oil pressure and water temperature gauges, finished off by a boost gauge for the Supercharger on the far right. Along with most of them, the Hobson telegauge for the fuel level does not work. The Blower car does not have pressure feed to the tank, being fitted with electric pumps. The gearbox is the 'D' type, with the standard, short stainless steel lever. The lever is more of a stretch than the 3-Litre, requiring a definite push forward into third.

Starting procedure is the same as the 3-Litre, without the need to pump up the pressure feed; instead, one simply switches on the pumps. The deep burble of the Blower is louder than the 3-Litre, with a harder edge to it – the silencer looked rather like a relic from the ark. The noise from the engine (all 4-cylinder Bentleys are noisy, compared to the 6-cylinder cars) is overlaid by the whistling from the carburettors, which is really rather unobtrusive. Once behind the wheel, the car could be a standard 4½-Litre. Nothing about the car from the driver's viewpoint gives the game away that it is the Supercharged model – the view down the bonnet, wider and flatter than the 3-Litre, is the same as a standard 4½-Litre. This impression is somewhat dispelled once the car is under way. The plate clutch of the Blower is no heavier than the cone clutch of the 3-Litre, and is just as easy in operation. The gear change, though, is quite different, despite the two cars having exactly the same gear ratios. I stalled the Supercharged car before realising that the supercharger has distinct throttle lag. Because of the length of the inlet pipe from the offside of the supercharger up to the inlet manifold, there is a distinct pause between depressing the throttle, and the desired increase in engine revolutions materialising. The other side of this, is that once the revs have gone up, they continue to rise briefly after you have taken your foot off the loud pedal because the compressed mixture is still rising up the inlet pipe! These

characteristics encourage a slightly different style of driving.

The Supercharged car GH 1932, was not run from the late 1950s until 1989. Tim Scott shipped the car back from its former home in Illinois, to Dick Moss, who says 'We cleaned the sump out with Redex, stuck back the bits of fabric that were coming off, cleaned it up a bit and set it up a bit rich as the cooling on a Blower is rather marginal. If I'd known how he was going to drive it … ' Tim Scott: 'If you put your foot down at about 70, the boost comes in like a turbo … it did about 5 miles per gallon all the way from Bedford to Nottingham!' Ted Parkinson, after driving it: 'I want one – I want one now!'

'Perhaps a suitable axiom for the Blowers might be, if Royce will forgive the misquotation: "The legends remain long after the unreliability is forgotten!" '
(T.D. Houlding, BDC *Review*, May 1983).

Cockpit of Ted Scott's very original Supercharged car. Placing the speedo on the far left was common. Speedos had a reputation for unreliability in the early years of the century, drivers preferring to see the rev counter, which is centrally placed. In this car, the speedo and rev counter are Jaeger chronometric; there should be a matching Jaeger clock on the far left.

bw3

Basically, the car likes more revs than the 3-Litre before changing up, and because of the extra mass of the engine/supercharger unit, the change is slightly slower. At first, this seems no problem, until you glance at the speedometer – and realise how quickly speed builds up. There is no sensation of drama, but the car has terrific poke, and you soon find that you are travelling very quickly. At 60, the boost gauge reads about zero (boost gauges were not fitted as standard, and this one is War Department surplus!), and Tim assures me that above 60, the car really motors, as the boost comes in. Under normal conditions, the power of the Supercharger shows up in the fact that the car can be driven in top under conditions that would really require the use of a lower gear in the 3-Litre. It was noticeable when following Ted in the 3-Litre that he had to change down on inclines that the Blower would happily stroll up in top gear. The supercharger appears to act as a clutch stop, and I would have to admit to finding the Blower the more difficult of the two. I think that much of this is due to the fact that the gearbox of the Supercharged car was less worn than that of

the 3-Litre, and is generally less forgiving. With practice, I think that the car would give enormous pleasure.

The steering is lower geared than the 3-Litre, but still feels heavier and slightly less responsive. It is difficult to tell whether it is heavier than a standard $4\frac{1}{2}$-Litre – psychologically, the mass over the front axle would say that it is, but it is very difficult to judge objectively. The extra length of the car does make it feel more unwieldy at low speed. One has to take the steering wheel firmly in hand and not be apologetic about it, and driven in that manner both cars become extremely satisfying. The steering is improved by judicious use of the throttle in corners. The Supercharged car has a completely standard braking set-up, with the self-wrapping front brakes. The pedal travel is much less than the 3-Litre, and although the pedal pressures without the servo of the smaller car were higher, I felt that the brakes were better, and was happier driving the Supercharged car slightly faster and slightly closer to the other traffic. Considering some of the comments made in the past, the Supercharged car is suprisingly smooth and sophisticated. The addition of

The Blower in open country. The angle of the front wheels is not deceptive – they really are meant to be like that!

GH1932

the Supercharger gives more damping to the engine, which along with the heavier crankshaft renders the engine quieter and smoother than the standard 4½-Litre.

The character of the two cars is so different from driving a modern car that at no time did I commit the cardinal error of wrong footing, and forgetting the central accelerator. However, when I drove David Sparrow's Citroen briefly during the photographic session, I accidentally wrong-footed in that – fortunately at low speed in a car park, without incident!

Obviously, as discussed in the Owner's Views, both cars have their drawbacks. It has to be borne in mind that both were exceedingly expensive when new, and are singularly lacking in creature comforts. Admittedly, had one wanted greater luxury, one would have bought a closed-bodied car when new – although closed 4-cylinder Bentleys can be rather noisy and unpleasant inside. It is unfortunate for the Blower car that it was produced at the end of the 1920s, when customer choice was changing in favour of smoother, 6-cylinder cars with greater comfort and an increasing emphasis on metal-panelled closed coachwork. The worst feature

of the Bentley car in general is undoubtedly the gearbox, which if it was as easy as some of the boxes made by rival manufacturers, such as Hispano-Suiza, would make the car a joy even to the uninitiated. It is easy to be intimidated by it, but provided one does not use force, the occasional noises do not seem to do any harm.

In summary, both cars have considerable charm, and the earlier, smaller, car stands up well against the Supercharged car. The 3-Litre would be slower over a distance, but possibly more relaxing to drive, because it requires less effort. Driven hard over give-and-take roads, it is possible that the Supercharged car's performance advantage would be nullified to a considerable extent. Both cars are so close to their original specification that they are, as near as is possible to get, representative of their type when new. Which would I choose to live with? I suppose the answer is really rather obvious – the Supercharged car, for it's greater room and comfort, and the fascination of it's effortless high-speed touring performance. I have a sneaking suspicion, though, that I'd overdo it some day....

PRIDE OF POSSESSION

Autofolio

51

Why a Bentley? Ted Parkinson – 'I've always had Bentleys, but in the reverse order from the usual: I started with an 8-Litre tourer, then bought a 4½-Litre with a two-seat body whilst owning the 8, and then sold the 4½ and swopped the 8-Litre for this 3-Litre earlier this year. The engine of the 8 was getting rather tired, and I didn't really fancy having it rebuilt.'
Tim Scott – 'I'd always wanted a Bentley, but it wasn't until other things had sorted themselves out that I went seriously looking for one. I decided that I wanted a supercharged car, so I researched the fifty cars looking for suitable ones. With such a small number of cars, the choice is inevitably somewhat limited. I bought this one from Dick Stitt in Illinois after long negotiations. I then managed to buy another one in

the UK, fitted with a rather special Vanden Plas open body, which is being rebuilt by Dick Moss.'

This led into a rather more general discussion.

'The Bentley is a very practical car. Generally they run for long periods with a minimum of attention, unlike, for example, a Bugatti, some of which are supposed to need an engine rebuild every five thousand miles.'

'Of course, the best place for a Bentley is France. WO definitely had French roads in mind when designing the car, and it is a great touring car.'

'The real disadantage of the Blower is it's petrol consumption – down to 5 mpg when driven hard. One firm recently found when thinking of using a Blower for a record run that the fuel consumption made it

impractical – down to 2 mpg at racing speeds! They couldn't get a big enough tank onto the track, as it would have needed a special licence.'

'The 3-Litre is rather better – about 18–20 mpg on a run. The original 11 gallon tank is rather meagre, consisting of 9 gallons and then a 2 gallon reserve brought into operation by a lever on the tank. There is no petrol gauge, so it helps if you carry a dipstick. And don't run the car on unleaded, as the valve seats are not hardened. The valve seats are several inches down the block with its non-detachable head, and inserting valve seats is very problematical.'

'The Blower has a 16 gallon tank, with a Hobson Telegauge. The Telegauge uses a long tube from the tank that translates to a column of red fluid in a gauge on the dashboard, but it is rare to find one that works these days. The last few Blowers were fitted with a 25 gallon tank as standard, for obvious reasons.'

'Possibly the worst feature of the 3-Litre is the Smith's headlamps. These just cast a yellow pool in front of the car, and are really rather hopeless. Most cars have had the Smith's headlights taken off and replaced by more efficient units – often Marchal, Zeiss or Lucas.'

'The Blower would have had Smith's from new, larger than those on the 3-Litre, but these were changed for Bosch in 1933.'

'The problem with additional lighting is the capacity of the dynamo. I drove a 3-Litre recently with vast Zeiss lights, and when these were turned on, the ammeter flicked immediately over to full discharge at –20 amps! The Smiths dynamo only pushes out 8 amps, which means that if you do a lot of night driving it is possible to find the lights gradually failing as the battery discharges. The common solution is to fit a bigger battery.'

'The other problem with the 3-Litre is the Autovac. These normally work perfectly, as long as the needle valves are moving freely. The Autovac uses the suction from the inlet manifold to allow atmospheric pressure to push the fuel through from the tank. This works fine under normal conditions, although you can dry up the Autovac on long climbs, and it is not suitable for racing. The Team cars had pressure feed, which this car has as well. However, the brake servo (which is non-standard) also uses the suction from the inlet manifold. This seems to upset the Autovac, so I never use it.'

'The Supercharged car has twin electric pumps, the only Vintage Bentley model to be so fitted. The Autopulses, of American origin, were used on the Team

Extracts from Bentley Motors Service Records for 3-Litre YM 83: Chassis PH 1462 1926 Speed. Guarantee expires 10/3/31 Vanden Plas 4-seater. Engine PH 1459 18 gallon petrol tank, pressure and Autovac feed to carburettors. Cambridge thermometer AT rev counter corded road springs, Duralumin valve rockers. Delivered to C.R. Robinson. 29/7/30 engine tuned for speed. 8/8/32 vacuum servo motor fitted. 15/3/34 Car tested max speed 92 mph (3500 rpm). Max temp 70°.

Extracts from Bentley Motors Service Records for 4½-Litre Supercharged GH 1932: Chassis SM 3913 1930 4½-Litre S.C. Final Test 21/7/30 Guarantee expires 26/7/35 Vanden Plas Sports 4-seater. Engine SM 3916.13/46 axle ratio. 'D' type gearbox 7219. 10ft 10½in WB. Berrys rear springs/Woodhead front. Large bore Pullswell silencer BM4092. BM4346/4 reinforced sump. Delivered to G.B. Sanderson by Rossleigh's, Edinburgh. 5.0 compression ratio-B&D friction shock absorbers. 28/8/33 Bosch headlamps fitted.

Speed Sixes in later years as well.'

'On the 8-Litre, the capacity of the Autovac was pushed right up to a gallon, for the bigger engine. The fuel consumption of the 8-Litre, though, is lower than that of the Blower – maybe 8 mpg under normal use.'

'The size of the car is deceptive – the 3-Litre looks big, but at 13 ft 3 in long by 5 ft 8 in wide it is really quite small. It is high, though, with a nice commanding driving position. It is deceptive, for example, when driving the 8-Litre or one of the longer 6½-Litres, the way the car shrinks around you. The only disconcerting aspect of the 8-Litre is that when going over a rise, the huge radiator seems to block out any

White House Corner, Le Mans, 1927? No, Ted Parkinson, somewhere on the Isle of Wight, 1989. This does show off the lines of the car, with the outside battery mounted on the nearside running board. The general appearance of this car is virtually identical to the 1926 and 1927 Le Mans 3-Litres, with the exception of the windscreen and petrol tank.

view of the road ahead!' 'The steering on the Blower is heavy, but very responsive, with about $1\frac{1}{4}$ turns from lock to lock.'

'The 3-Litre is lighter, but even higher geared at 1 turn from lock to lock. The car is running on 5.25 x 21 in wheelrim Dunlops, but with a high-ratio steering box that was intended to be fitted with the narrow, high-pressure beaded edge tyres. On those the steering would be sensational – just like a bicycle.'

'Although the steering on the Blower is heavier, it doesn't seem to be any heavier than that of the $4\frac{1}{2}$-Litre – despite the weight of the Blower over the front axle.'

'The Blower car is suprisingly sophisticated, considering its reputation. The ride is really rather smooth and comfortable. It is arguable that the Blower car is the best of the lot, as it has the characteristics and size of the $4\frac{1}{2}$-Litre with the performance of the Speed Six.'

'The 6-cylinder Bentleys do feel bigger than the 4-cylinder cars, with the exception of Bill Lake's Team Speed Six. That car is the only 6-cylinder Bentley I've driven that really felt like a $4\frac{1}{2}$-Litre, but with tremendous performance. It's easy to forget that a well set-up road-going Speed Six should be capable of getting on for 120 mph, and a Blower should be able

to do the same. After all, the Birkin single-seater must have been doing about 150 in a straight line.'

'The usual adage is that you start with a 3-Litre, and then move up to a $4\frac{1}{2}$-Litre. By the time you can afford a Speed Six, you're too old and unfit to drive it!'

'The springing on the 3-Litre is good, but when new the springs were corded, it would have had the effect of stiffening up the suspension at the expense of comfort.'

'Cording the springs would probably increase the ultimate cornering abilities of the car – a friend of mine raced his standard $4\frac{1}{2}$-Litre at Goodwood, and found when pushing it that the car would hop neatly sideways. Totally safe and predictable, but when cornering hard the car would suddenly be a couple of feet to one side but pointing in exactly the same direction.'

'Spares and repairs are no real problem – they just cost money! There is a small service industry that has sprung up around the cars, and virtually all the mechanical components can be bought. It is even possible to buy a virtually complete new engine. However, with the current high values of the cars, restoration costs tend to be in proportion.'

'As the cars were hand fitted, jobs tend to be far more time-consuming than they would be on a modern car. The cars were of course designed with a rather different principle in mind, that of repair rather than replacement. Fortunately, so far they have proved endlessly repairable, and you won't find such 'modern' tricks as shafts running direct in housings without bushes.'

Above right *It has to be remembered that the Birkin cars were built with just one end in mind – to win at Le Mans. In this they were, of course, unsuccessful, but that does not detract from the almost brutal functional nature of the beast. In those days, real racing cars had bigger steering wheels, not smaller as the modern fashion. With the weight of the steering, the bigger wheels were used for more leverage, and the Bentleys are as physical to drive as might be imagined from their looks. The steering wheels on the Birkin team cars were another 2 inches bigger in diameter than that shown here.*

'The gearboxes seem to go on and on, although some have had to be rebuilt with new gears – you know you have a problem when it jumps out of gear on a steep hill.'

'The gearbox of the 3-Litre is definitely rather on the musical side!'

'Possibly the weak point of the design is the back axle, particularly the early two-star design with the aluminium cage. The later four-star, with the cast iron cage, is better, but the cages eventually break up. The very late cars used a steel alloy cage. The solution really is preventative maintenance. Stripping and rebushing a two star diff every 50,000 miles would probably make it run for ever, and similarly rebuilding a four star every 100,000 miles.'

'A quiet back axle is not necessarily a good one – it has been known for a silent axle to have a tooth off the pinion, or the cage cracked in several places.'

'The crownwheel and pinions are funny. The 14/53 ratio, standard on the 3-Litre Speed Model, seems to be the only one susceptible to teeth dropping off the pinion. It is the only standard ratio for the 4-cylinder cars with an even number of teeth on the pinion – the others have 13 or 15 teeth – so perhaps there is a reason?'

'Tyres are readily available as well, the problem is paying for them, at about £100 a cover plus tube.'

'The bottom line is that the cars are terrific fun to drive, and that's what really matters.'

Supercharged 4½-Litre

The Supercharged 4½-Litre used a derivative of the Standard 4½-Litre chassis, and was generally very similar.

Chassis 35 ton. 188 inch pressed steel, ladder frame with four pressed cross-members and bolted strut gear. Track 4 ft 8 in. Width 5 ft 8½ in. Wheelbase 10 ft 10 in. Overall length 14 ft 7 in.

Chassis weights 28½ cwt (without coachwork); 34 cwt with open coachwork, 38½ cwt closed coachwork (maximum weights allowed under terms of the Five Year Guarantee).

Brakes On all 4 wheels, mechanically operated. 400 mm diameter drums. Self-wrapping ('semi servo') front brakes (basically a single leading shoe design).

Front Axle H-section 40 ton tensile steel. Heavy pattern beam. Some chassis fitted with beam with integral jacking lugs.

Rear Axle Welded pressed steel construction, semi-floating underslung. 13/46 (3.53:1) ratio, 15/50 (3.3:1) to order. Speed Six pattern differential, 4-star.

Suspension Semi-elliptic leaf springs, various numbers of leaves depending on body weight. Woodhead front springs, Berry rear. André shock-absorbers.

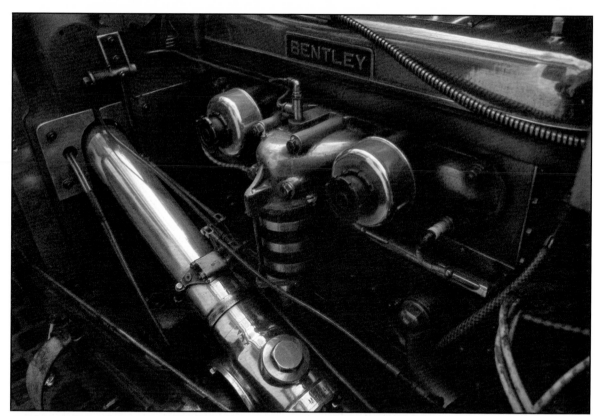

Gearbox 4-speed and reverse, right-hand gate change. 'D' type close ratio, no syncromesh.

Clutch Single dry-plate.

Transmission Spicer shaft.

Wheels and tyres 6.00 in x 21 in Rudge-Whitworth centre lock, Dunlop wellbase covers.

Steering Worm and wheel. 10.3:1 ratio. Bluemel sprung wheel.

Radiator German silver shell. Label white on black. Thicker core than standard 4½-Litre, cut away at bottom.

Engine 4-cylinder non-detachable head. Crankshaft and camshaft in five main bearings each, white metal lined. 100x140 mm, 4398 cc. Four valves per cylinder. Forged steel crank (crankshaft weight 75 lb opposed to 47 lb of standard shaft). Heavy pattern cylinder block and crankcase, etc. Aluminium alloy pistons. Compression ratio; 4.5:1, or 5.0:1. 175 bhp at 3500 rpm, 182 bhp at 3900 rpm.

Valve gear Single overhead camshaft, driven by bevel gears. Duralumin rockers in rocker boxes (forked inlet, two single exaust).

Ignition Twin Bosch FF4 or FU4B magnetos. Firing order 1-3-4-2. Two plugs per cylinder. Smiths dynamo and starter.

Supercharger Amherst Villiers Mk IV Roots type. Boost 9½ lbs at 3500 rpm, 10 lbs at 3900 rpm. (Up to 12 lbs boost on Birkin cars.) Triple blow-off valves. Plain case SM 3901–SM 3925, ribbed case MS 3926–MS 3950.

Petrol system – 16 gallon rear tank, with twin electric pumps (Autopulses). 25 gallon tank chassis MS 3941 on.

Lamps Smiths or Lucas, to customer choice.

Instruments Very much to order. These would normally include the Bentley Motors switchplate with the chassis number engraved, Jaeger speedometer and rev counter, Smiths bezel switch/ammeter, clock and oil pressure gauge, and a Hobson Telegauge petrol gauge. Larger 'Team Car' speedometers and rev counters were available to order, as were any additional instruments the customer desired. Neither a temperature gauge nor a boost gauge were fitted as standard.

Worm's eye view, or mechanic's view from the ramp! This is the back of the Supercharged car, on the off-side. In the centre of the picture is the battery box. In the days of chassis manufacturers, there was inevitably some overlap between the manufacturer and the coachbuilder as to who made some of the detail fittings. On the 3-Litres, early 6½- and 4½-Litres, the battery was generally positioned outside the frame, in all but the very early years in some sort of Bentley Motors-made construction. The coachbuilder then had to build around this, or move the battery altogether if he wished. Hanging the battery inside the chassis is better from an engineering viewpoint, and makes the coachbuilder's job easier, and that is what Bentleys did on all models from 1929 on.

Birkin cars

The specification of the Birkin cars was much that of the standard cars, with special 45 gallon fuel tanks, stoneguards, extra scuttle-mounted oil tank, and a host of special details for racing.

This view shows the massive plate clutch of the Supercharged car, and the clutch shaft back to the gearbox. Although making the engine and gearbox in one unit was not uncommon in those days, Bentleys preferred to stick to a separate gearbox driven by a short Cardan shaft. The fabric disc is a Hardy coupling, which gives a degree of flexibility to the drive.

Side view of the sump. On the late cars, Bentleys made more and more use of Elektron for their castings. Elektron is a magnesium alloy, stronger and lighter than aluminium. The problem with Elektron is the difficulty of preventing corrosion. It is far more susceptible to corrosion than aluminium, and, other than spraying regularly with oil, very difficult to maintain.

Clutch/gearbox of the Supercharged car. The gearbox, on the left, is the close-ratio D box. The pedal shaft runs in aluminium blocks bolted to the chassis rail, incorporating a spherical steel ball. The spherical ball allows movement of the shaft relative to the ever-flexing frame.

Visible here is the dumb-iron and the spring shackle, and the long, semi-elliptic leaf spring. Long springs were used to give better riding characteristics, as the suspension had very limited travel, much of the movement being in the frame itself. The pipe in the top centre is the petrol filler neck.

HISTORIES OF THE SUPERCHARGED BENTLEYS

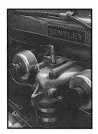

Chassis SM 3901-SM 3925.

**SM 3901 SM 3906 GF 776 Apr 30 4-SEATER VdP
SIR D LEWIS.**
'Chromium plated radiator and large bore silencer. 8 Litre type exhaust cut out fitted 22/1/31 and Le Mans type petrol tank 9/1/33.' Believed to have been broken up, and parts built into other cars.

**SM 3902 SM 3905 PO 3265 Dec 30 SALOON F&W
MISS E.M. UNWIN**
'2 door grey fabric Sportsman's Saloon. 6½-Litre pattern steering controls fitted, racing type accelerator pedal. 15 gallon tank converted to 20 gallon 7/10/31.' Freestone & Webb Olympia Show car (1929). Now in Australia, with Vanden Plas replica body.

**SM 3903 SM 3907 UW 3761 Oct 29 4-SEATER VdP
J. WESTON ADAMSON**
'Showroom demonstrator. Gearbox modified to central change 12/2/32.' Bentley Motors Olympia Show car (1929). Was in Australia – now back in the UK. Converted back to right-hand change.

**SM 3904 SM 3908 PL 1150 Jul 30 4-SEATER VdP
J.S. HINDMARSH**
'20″ steering wheel. Accident 29/8/32; salvage purchased by BM Ltd. Car rebuilt; fitted engine SM 3904.' Rebuilt with Corsica body and unsupercharged engine, now in Sweden.

**SM 3905 SM 3904 EU 919 Apr 30 SALOON (W) MTN
CAPT D'ARCY HALL**
'Chrome plated fittings. Large dial Jaeger speedo and enlarged type silencer fitted 21/6/30.' Rebuilt as Le Mans replica by Elmdown, now in Sweden.

**SM 3906 SM 3912 GH 1808 Jul 30 D/H COUPE GN
H.N. HOLDER**
'Chrome plated parts, exhaust cut out with outside pipe attached. Rear hand and footbrake shoes coupled together. 2″ longer steering column with 20″ wheel – cam action radiator filler cap. Le Mans type accelerator fitted 5/4/33. 264 lbs ballast to rear compartment fitted 2/1/34.' Driven in Monte Carlo Rally – retired. Now in USA with Vanden Plas four-seat body.

**SM 3907 SM 3909 GK 8445 Jun 30 4-SEATER VdP
R.T. RICHARDS**
'Grebel spotlight fitted 16/3/31. 1/5/31 – parts sent to Paris Depot. 14/5/31 – compression plate sent to owner in Greece. Exported to Australia 1939.' Rebuilt in Australia with Vanden Plas style tourer by Ward.

**SM 3908 SM 3911 GF 7875 May 30 4-SEATER VdP
CAPT WYNDHAM**
'15/50 axle ratio.' Supercharger removed and saloon body fitted 1948. Now in Caister Motor Museum, with original body and another supercharger fitted.

**SM 3909 SM 3910 GK 6661 Jul 30 2-SEATER GN
WOOLF BARNATO**
'Large bore silencer, chrome plated parts. Supercharger changed for ribbed type 11/2/31. Engine tuned for hill-climb – Le Mans accelerator fitted 31/3/31. 7/7/31 4.58 axle fitted. 11/9/31 original 3.53 axle fitted.' Now in America.

**SM 3910 SM 3913 GH 2830 Jul 30 4-SEATER VdP
J.W. LEWIS**
'Large bore silencer – 33x6.00 tyres.' No supercharger fitted at present – car in USA.

**SM 3911 SM 3914 DV 7611 Dec 30 COUPE MTN
H.F.W. PRINCE**
'Maythorn & Sons secondhand coupé. 17/8/37 Dismantled after accident. Reassembled and tested.' Rebodied as open tourer – believed dismantled after head-on crash.

**SM 3912 SM 3915 GH 21 Aug 30 2-SEATER PH
BROUGHAM & VAUX**
'Reinforced sump. Chrome plated parts. No bonnet. Steering column 2″ longer than standard. Large bore silencer. Accident 21/5/35 – chassis frame reconditioned, new rear axle banjo, petrol tank and front axle reconditioned, etc. 2 reconditioned Zeiss headlamps fitted.' Not heard of since 1939.

**SM 3913 SM 3916 GH 1932 Jul 30 4-SEATER VdP
G.B. SANDERSON**
'Reinforced sump, large bore Pullswell silencer and aluminium diff centre. Accident 25/1/33 – chassis frame reconditioned, new front axle bed fitted. Bosch

headlamps fitted 28/8/33. 25 gallon tank fitted 19/3/36.'

SM 3914 SM 3917 GK 3840 Oct 30 COUPE VdP J. HOWARTH

'Speedo gears to give 4% fast reading. Chrome plated parts. Registered GK 3840 then SG1 then DS 2123. Accident 19/12/34 – chassis frame checked and reconditioned back axle banjo fitted.' Vanden Plas Olympia Show car (1930). Rebodied as Le Mans replica, chassis cut to 9 ft 9½in wheelbase. In Scandinavia.

SM 3915 SM 3919 HOLLAN Oct 30 2/3-SEATER GN E. HERTZBERGER

'Chrome plated parts, large bore Pullswell silencer. 14/9/31 experimental brake adjuster sent to owner. 26/9/31 6½-Litre type steering column controls fitted. Racing type brake adjuster fitted. Bought in as scrap.' [By Bentley Motors Co. 1935]. Body copied from SM 3909.

SM 3916 SM 3922 GK 8443 Oct 30 2/3-SEATER GN S.B. PECK

'Chrome plated parts large bore Pullswell silencer. Bosch headlamps fitted 25/9/35.' Body copied from SM 3909. Now in America.

SM 3917 MS 3933 GH 6951 Aug 30 4-SEATER VdP P. CHANDLER

'Showroom demonstrator. Chrome plated parts and large bore silencer.' In the UK – one owner since 1940.

SM 3918 SM 3920 GK 150 Sep 30 4-SEATER VdP T. HEATON

'Le Mans type s/c chassis. 42 gallon tank. Split-pinned all round. 3 mm off cylinder base.' In UK.

SM 3919 SM 3923 GX 8727 Mar 31 4-SEATER GN DUKE OF LEINSTER

'Chrome plated parts – large bore Pullswell silencer. Stock [sold 1932].' Rebuilt by Moss – now in Sweden.

SM 3920 SM 3924 GK 3841 Nov 30 4-SEATER VdP R. KERSHAW

'33x6.00 tyres, chrome plated parts. 5 brush dynamo and twin Bosch horns fitted 17/12/30.' Bentley Motors Olympia Show car (1930). In Switzerland.

SM 3921 SM 3918 VM 404 Jun 31 SALOON (W) F&W W. PROCTOR-SMITH

'Panelled Weymann saloon – stock to Showrooms. Chrome plated parts.' Probably broken up – chassis frame in MS 3930.

SM 3922 MS 3926 GK 8837 Nov 30 4-SEATER VdP E. LEIGH

'Stock to Showrooms. Accident 31/3/31 – reconditioned front axle bed fitted. Supercharger rotor case changed 5/3/32.' In UK – now registered BD40.

SM 3923 SM 3925 KR 7989 Dec 30 4-SEATER VdP T.M. BEST DALISON

'R.T. silencer, exhaust cut-out. Andre tele-control shock absorbers. Chrome plated parts.' Still in UK.

SM 3924 MS 3927 GO 2641 Jan 31 4-SEATER VdP G.C. HEYWOOD

'Chrome plated parts – speedo drive gears giving 4 per cent fast reading. New steering wheel supplied by owner fitted 7/7/32.' Cut to 9 ft 9½ in wheelbase and rebuilt as Le Mans replica.

SM 3925 MS 3928 GW 2222 Jun 31 SALOON (W)F&W T. BYRON

'Panelled Weymann saloon – Showrooms. Sold by Jack Barclays with one year guarantee. Lucas P100 headlamps fitted 22/2/33. Accident 24/6/35 – chassis frame reconditioned and new front axle bed fitted. Reconditioned D box sent to Howes Garage 8/11/38.' Engine now in a 3-Litre.

Chassis MS 3926-MS 3950.

MS 3926 MS 3929 GO 1400 Apr 31 4-SEATER VdP T.G. MOORE

'Chrome plated parts. Accident 1/12/31 – front axle reconditioned. 15/6/32 – accident due to fire.' Was registered GMN 578 in Isle of Man; now in USA.

MS 3927 MS 3930 GP 1993 Apr 31 4-SEATER VdP O.D. WINTERBOTTOM

'Stock to Showrooms – chrome plated parts.' Now in USA.

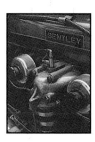

MS 3928 SM 3921 FG 6667 Mar 31 D/H COUPE GN
GORDON BLACK
'Chrome plated parts – 4 per cent fast reading speedo gears.' Rebuilt as Le Mans replica – now in USA.

MS 3929 MS 3932 JB 1850 -/33 4-SEATER VdP
A. ANSELL
'Vanden Plas for storage.' [Apparently not sold until 1933]. Now in USA.

MS 3930 MS 3935 YY 3692 Apr 31 4-SEATER VdP
W. ESPLEN
'Stock to Showrooms. Accident 4/6/36 – chassis frame reconditioned. Front axle bed reconditioned. Reconditioned back axle banjo fitted.' Currently being rebuilt as Le Mans replica.

MS 3931 MS 3931 FS 1179 May 31 SALOON (W) GN
JAMES F. BRYSON
'Chrome plated parts. Weymann close-coupled saloon. Engine no MR 3391 [unsupercharged $4\frac{1}{2}$-Litre engine] fitted by Bowlers of Alperton, August 1936. Registered FS 1179 then AGH 10 then UW 6441.' Last heard of 1956.

MS 3932 MS 3936 GN 6087 May 31 4-SEATER VdP
B.W. PRESTON
'Jack Barclay Ltd sale or return. Chrome plated parts, 4 per cent fast speedo gears. $6\frac{1}{2}$-Litre type controls fitted 11/1/31. Accident 27/2/33 – chassis frame reconditioned. Steering column assembly lengthened 3″ 30/4/36.' Original engine in Pacey-Hassan Special. MS 3932 currently being rebuilt and rebodied.

MS 3933 MS 3934 GX 8870 Jun 31 4-SEATER VdP
WOOLF BARNATO
'Chrome plated parts – ally nosepiece to back axle. [as opposed to Elektron].' Now in USA.

MS 3934 MS 3937 GY 3904 May 31 4-SEATER VdP
W.R. HANDLEY
'Chrome plated parts, ally nosepiece to back axle. 4 per cent fast speedo gears.' Fitted $6\frac{1}{2}$-Litre engine. Since restored with supercharged $4\frac{1}{2}$-Litre engine, as Le Mans replica on 9 ft $9\frac{1}{2}$ in wheelbase.

MS 3935 MS 3938 GK 8449 Jan 31 4-SEATER VdP
HUBERT MASON
'Chrome plated parts, ally nosepiece to back axle, exhaust downpipe lagged. Accident 30/5/33 – chassis frame and front axle bed reconditioned.' Currently being rebuilt.

MS 3936 MS 3939 GP 1630 Jun 31 COUPE LD
I.W. BIRTS
'Lancefield close-coupled saloon, chrome plated parts. 4 per cent fast speedo drive gears.' Rebuilt as Le Mans replica by Elmdown – in UK

MS 3937 MS 3942 GP 42 Jul 31 4-SEATER VdP
C.J.L. LANGLANDS
'1931 Le Mans type s/c chassis. Chromeplated parts and Smith's thermometer. Supercharger pressure gauge fitted.' Subsequently owned by Amherst Villiers in USA.

MS 3938 MS 3940 GT 8771 Sep 31 4-SEATER MFR
J.R. QUAYLE
'Chrome plated parts. Bentley & Draper friction and hydraulic shock-absorbers.' Rebuilt as Vanden Plas 4-seater registered AW2.

MS 3939 MS 3945 MV 297 Sep 31 4-SEATER VdP
H. OLSWANG
'Exhaust cut-out, engine thermometer and detachable stoneguard. Exported to South Africa.' Owner killed in car 1931. Rebodied with body off Model A Ford 1940 – subsequently rebodied as Vanden Plas tourer, still in South Africa.

MS 3940 MS 3943 JO 732 Nov 30 4-SEATER GN
MAHARAJAH OF INDORE
'Chrome plated parts. Exported to India.' Broken up – engine fitted to a speedboat; still at the bottom of Bombay Harbour.

MS 3941 MS 3944 GN 6090 May 31 4-SEATER VdP
MISS N. McCAW
'Chrome plated parts and ally nosepiece to back axle.' In museum in USA.

MS 3942 MS 3946 GT 8774 Jul 31 4-SEATER VdP
D.L. BAKER
'Chrome plated parts. Cambridge thermometer and 6 rev counter fitted 3/2/33.' Rebuilt and cut to 9 ft $9\frac{1}{2}$ in wheelbase 1946 – subsequently rebuilt as Le Mans replica, now in USA.

MS 3943 MS 3947 GX 555 Sep 31 D/H COUPE VdP
W.T. WILLMOTT
'25 gallon tank and Pullswell silencer.' Now in Sweden.

MS 3944 MS 3941 UR 6572 Jul 31 4-SEATER VdP
H. LEESON

'1931 4½-Litre s/c Le Mans chassis. Rev counter. Extra pair B&D hydraulic shock absorbers to rear. 25 gallon tank. Special clutch stop plate.' Rebodied as two-seater by Johnson in 1938. In USA.

MS 3945 MS 3950 GY 4300 Aug 31 D/H COUPE VdP
L.S. CARLYLE

'Chrome plated parts, rev counter and Pullswell silencer.' Probably broken up – parts built into other cars.

MS 3946 MS 3948 GY 3905 Aug 31 D/H COUPE VdP
MAJ C.L.Y. PARKER

'VdP sportsman's coupé, black with grey leather upholstery. 24/1/33 Bosch headlamps fitted. 5/4/38 straight-tooth 15/46 back axle gears.' Rebuilt as Le Mans replica by Elmdown on 9 ft 9½ in chassis. Now in the National Motor Museum.

MS 3947 MS 3952 GX 6170 Sep 31 D/H COUPE VdP
G. BEEBY

'10/2/33 Supercharger removed – converted to standard [unsupercharged 4½-Litre]. SU carbs and manifold fitted. Supercharger cowl modified.' Rebuilt as Le Mans replica by Elmdown, fitted ex-Birkin supercharger.

MS 3948 MS 3951 GY 7847 Sep 31 D/H COUPE VdP
E.G. TITLEY

'Chrome parts, rev counter and Pullswell silencer. 15/6/34 – owner's Jaeger rev counter fitted.' Rebuilt with Vanden Plas style body by Robinson.

MS 3949 MS 3949 DS 240 Sep 31 D/H COUPE VdP
J.H. VANDER HEIDE

'Exported to Holland 1933 – returned to UK 1935 registered BGH 55.' Rebuilt as two-seater by Nayland – subsequently rebuilt as Le Mans replica by Elmdown.

MS 3950 MS 3953 GY 7846 Sep 31 D/H COUPE VdP
A. STORKEY

'24/8/33 Supercharger removed, converted to standard 4½-Litre.' Rebuilt as Le Mans replica with supercharger – now in Sweden.

Notes

The columns are: chassis number, engine number, original UK registration number, date of delivery, body style, coachbuilder, and first owner. The subsequent comments in inverted commas are from the Bentley Service Records.
Coachbuilders:

F&W	Freestone & Webb
GN	Gurney Nutting
LD	Lancefield
MFR	Mayfair
MTR	Maythorn
PH	Phillips
VdP	Vanden Plas

PHOTO SESSIONS

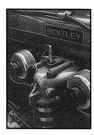

To spend two days in cold November driving around the Isle of Wight in order to have your car photographed for someone else's book takes a special kind of person. When that car is a Bentley, worth the sort of money that these are, 'special' could easily be replaced with words like 'odd' or 'lunatic'. Could easily; but when author Michael Hay and I met owner Ted Parkinson prior to boarding the ferry, it was apparent that here was a man with endless patience. Put a Bentley in a ferry queue, and all and sundry leave their cars to come and gawk and prod – and ask questions. How many times I heard Ted answer the same questions I cannot count – but only because I ran out of fingers. It was the same in the queue on the return journey, except that we had Tim Scott with his 4½-Litre as well, and coachloads came to prod and gawk and ask the same questions. Neither Ted nor Tim showed anything but politeness and pleasure in answering them. On the photo sessions they were sometimes less polite – taking childish delight in engulfing me with their cars' deadly black fumes whenever I asked them to move. Anyway, my throat's better now; the pleasure of having worked with these two charming 'special' people is something I will always remember. I thank you both. Also on the Isle of Wight I must thank Alan Parker and Chris Hynes of Arreton Valley Nursery Ltd for the short-notice use of their beautiful grounds. The Isle of Wight Railway's Terry Hastings was also most helpful indeed, as were all the staff at Carisbrooke Castle, especially John Paton.

Special thanks are due to Ian Wiltshire, and his second-in-command Colin Westbury, of the Halfway Service Station, where secure lodgings for the two cars were found, and where the use of a hydraulic ramp was provided so that detail shots could be photographed in a civilised manner.

The photo session of the Birkin Replica was arranged thanks to Stanley Mann, who loaned the car for the day along with Michael Brisby to look after and drive it. The latter was thoroughly nice to me the entire time, although he does have the unnerving habit of dropping Leonard Cohen lyrics into otherwise normal conversations. Thanks go to the oft-frozen model, Sarah Ward; and to the Haberdashers' Aske's School and Elstree Aerodrome for the locations.

The final photo session involved Harry Booth's Blower and was arranged thanks to the kindness of the owner and the helpfulness of Coys of Kensington, in whose showrooms the car resided. Thanks also go to Coys' willing pushers, Lara and Dorothy – stalwarts both!

For those interested in such matters, colour film was all Kodachrome; 25, 64 and 200 ASA (including 120). Black & white film was Kodak T-MAX TMX and TMY, 35 mm and 120 mm. 35 mm taken with two Leica R4 cameras with lenses from 16 mm to 560 mm. 120 system was Hasselblad, 38 to 150 mm lenses. My cat's name is Boris.

David Sparrow